SECURITY CHALLENGEs: 1

Book 1: A novel based on the true story of the first 22 years (1949–1971) of the life of a Samoan boy.

Volume 1

PASENE TAUIALO

ISBN: 13:978-0-6486679-0-2

Independently Published by Pasene Tauialo

Dedication

I dedicate this book to:

my parents – Iutita and Tauialo-o-Lilomaiava Faámausili;

my grandma Lumepa Lilo Sakalia;

my brothers and sisters Fomaí, Semu, Pina, Filemu, Luka, Lili, Fomaí;

my wife Tumema;

my children Ali'itasi Agamalu, Aperaámo and wife Yoland, Iutita Elenoa, Olive and husband Anton Punivai; and

my grandchildren Joshua, Noah, Elijah, Roman, and those to come.

May you all glorify the great Love of the Lord – the security in this world

Table of Contents

Prologue

Tusi was born in Malaeafoa, a small village, on the island of Savai'i in Samoa, in the South Pacific. This is Tusi's story, based on true events and spanning the first 22 years (1949–1971) of his life in Samoa.

In the culture of Samoa, telling someone to go and eat chicken shit is an insult and can warrant a fine from the council of chiefs.

But a grandma telling her grandson that if he didn't work hard an alternative would be to eat chicken shit to survive was not an insult but an expression of her love. It was a wise incentive and a challenge for Tusi to work hard at school and on their plantation and to respond to the bullying and mocking he encountered as a child in a fruitful, peaceful and rewarding way. The council of chiefs did not fine Grandma for her words because she was innocent and wise.

For future security, Grandma and parents taught Tusi that he would need to work hard, try his best, and make the best use of whatever resources he had and opportunities he was given. They taught him that in all areas of life, people reap what they have sown. Alongside this, they taught him to believe that whatever he could not afford and could not do himself, God would provide and do everything that was needed.

Chapter One

Fed with words

Tusi loved playing physical sports anywhere, anytime. During a Saturday afternoon rugby game, six-year-old Tusi was involved in a fight. Iose hit Tusi's head with the coconut husk that they used as a rugby ball. After biting Iose's ear in retaliation, Tusi ran for his life home. On arriving home, Tusi stopped for a drink of water from the tap outside their house.

As he was drinking, a voice called, "Tusi, look here." He turned and was surprised to see his grandma in the house, holding a plate of something up in the air. Tusi ran and gave Grandma a hug and greeted her with a kiss on her cheek.

"This is your food son. Sit down and eat."

"Oh thanks, Grandma," answered Tusi, and he sat and enjoyed the tail of *eleni* (herring) fish and a ripe banana.

Grandma lived on the family's plantation which was about 40 kilometres inland from the seaside village that was home to Tusi. Every weekend, Grandma came to the village to attend church on Sunday. She wouldn't visit without bringing something for Tusi, her favourite grandson. She was very protective of him, especially when Tusi was in trouble with other children and getting the belt from his father. Unfortunately, these were common occurrences for Tusi.

"Do you like your *eleni* fish?" asked Grandma.

"Oh yes. It is nice. But…"

"But what?"

"But, why do we always eat *eleni* fish and not *pisupo* (corned beef) like the other families?" Tusi's friends often teased and mocked him because he ate *eleni* instead of *pisupo*.

"Well, *pisupo* is expensive. *Eleni* is much cheaper."

"Oh. So, when are we going to buy and eat *pisupo*?"

"When we get enough money."

"When will that be?"

"Son, if you work hard on the plantation with your father to plant more coconut, cocoa, ava, taro, and ta'amu and raise more pigs and chickens, we can then sell more of the produce in the shops to get money to buy any amount of expensive, mouth-watering *pisupo* you want."

"Work hard on the plantation! No Grandma, I hate plantation work."

"Son, if farming is hard then you must go to school, do well, and then get a good job to get plenty of money to buy any amount of *pisupo* you want."

"But Grandma, plantation work and school will take almost the whole day leaving no time for playing sports with my friends."

"Sports! I beg your pardon son! Did you say sports? Look son, in our village, you get no money, no *pisupo* or even *eleni* from the kind of sports you and your friends play. So, if you spend the whole day, every day of your life playing those sports, what then are you going to eat in future? Chicken shit?" shouted Grandma with big eyes focused on Tusi.

Grandma's voice had grown louder and higher. Tusi said, "Your voice is loud Grandma – are you angry with me?"

"I am not angry but concerned about your future. I raise my voice to make sure my teachings go through your ears and stick into your thick lazy head."

"Plantation! School! That is a very difficult life Grandma."

"Son, it is not difficult. All you need to do is have some *ake* (liver)."

"You mean *ake* (liver) like the pig liver we eat?"

"No, the liver I refer to is boldness or braveness or courage. You must have that courage to work hard on the plantation and at school. When you have that courage, all things including working on the plantation and school will be easy."

"But Grandma, I only have the liver to punch those kids if they keep on mocking me for eating *eleni* and not *pisupo*."

"Wait son, that is bad liver."

"Why?"

"First, fighting is not allowed in our village and because of your fighting our family may get big fines from the council of chiefs. Second, your liver to retaliate with a punch ends up in a black eye, not a plate of corned beef." As grandma continued Tusi touched his left eye, swollen and black from a fight with Sega. "Third, your courage to hit back will not stop the kids mocking you again, and fourth, boxing will never give you money to buy *pisupo*. So, you will still be eating *eleni*, if not chicken shit, given your love of sports."

As time went by, Grandma observed that Tusi was more and more often getting involved in fights with other children. So, one day, because of her concern, Grandma decided to take Tusi to spend some time with her on the plantation.

"I spoke with your parents and they agreed that you will come and spend a week on the plantation with me."

"But our plantation is too far (it was about 40 kilometres). I hate long walks especially to the plantation and with slow walkers like you."

"I know that but if we wake up early, say at the third crow of the roosters at dawn and start walking, we should be there well before noon."

On Monday morning, hearing the second crow of the roosters but thinking it was the third, Grandma woke up Tusi.

"This is too early Grandma. Everybody in the village is still sleeping and I am tired and very sleepy still."

"Son, this is the right time to start – a little extra sleep, a little folding of your hands to sleep will delay our trip and we may therefore be caught by the hot sun or rain along the way."

Tusi cursed to himself as he forced himself to get up. "Do I have the liver to do whatever? What a life!"

While Tusi walked with Grandma just before dawn, the moon was shining brightly, and the sky was full of moving patches of clouds. As these patches of clouds moved across the moon, their shadows also moved across the ground and the trees.

"You see Grandma, there are no people on the track besides us. Everyone else is still enjoying their sound sleep while we are walking with ghosts."

"Where are the ghosts?"

"Wait Grandma, one is coming – a big black one. Don't make any noise. Feel it? See, it is on us and it is moving towards the mountain now", whispered Tusi grabbing Grandma's hand tightly.

"Son, I don't feel anything besides you holding tightly to my hand but if you do feel something, then that is good experience because ghosts are everywhere", answered Grandma. Having some idea of what Tusi was referring to as ghosts, Grandma continued, "Ghosts come and go like moving clouds across the rays of moonlight. They attempt to frighten people from doing the right thing or tempt people to do all sorts of silly things. If you fear ghosts, they will keep frightening you but if you scare them then they will run away."

As Grandma spoke, Tusi looked at the sky and followed the shadows as the patches of clouds moved across the moon rays, "You are right Grandma. The ghosts are as big as the shadows of the clouds. Now I see."

"Yes, I am glad you have learnt something. Would you have experienced moving ghosts if you were still in bed like most of the people of the village, including those kids who mocked you?"

"I don't think so."

Tusi and Grandma had taken with them a small basket containing a breadfruit, a tin of fish, a small coconut shell of *vai* (water), and a box of matches. By sunrise, they had completed about 95 per cent of their journey. They sat down under a big mango tree for a drink and ate half of the breadfruit for breakfast. While eating, Tusi sighted a small bird on the pawpaw tree so he went after it with his slingshot. Slowly and quietly he stalked but was unsuccessful. However, instead of catching the bird he picked a large ripe pawpaw fruit from the tree.

Tusi was still hungry and he told Grandma that they were going to eat the fruit. "Oh, oh, we have a problem Grandma."

"What is the problem?"

"We forgot to bring our small knife."

"Son, are you telling me that without a knife you won't eat that ripe fruit and yet you are hungry?"

"What should I do?"

"Son, always think of an alternative. In this case, you don't need a knife, just crack the fruit into pieces on that big rock, remove the seeds with your fingers and eat the flesh."

Tusi followed her advice and they were soon enjoying the sweet fruit before continuing their journey.

As they climbed the hills, they came to a big fallen fig tree across the road and Grandma said, "Let us rest under the trunk of this fallen tree for a little while because the thick cloud overhead tells us that rain is coming very soon."

"What will we do if the rain keeps falling for the rest of the day? We don't even have an umbrella."

"Well, before the rain falls, we have to prepare an umbrella."

"How?"

"Son, I told you to always think about alternatives. You see those banana trees? Go and get two leaves."

"But remember, we forgot our knife Grandma?"

"You don't need a knife to cut a banana leaf."

"So, what shall I do?"

"How strong are your teeth?"

"Very strong."

"The stalks of banana leaves are soft so do you think you can use your teeth to cut the stalks?"

"I don't know but I think my liver says I can", replied Tusi. After cutting through the stalks with his teeth Tusi managed to get two leaves to use as their umbrellas for the rest of their trip.

Arriving at the plantation, Tusi and Grandma were exhausted. There was no more talking. Instead they lay down and rested in their small plantation hut. The hut was about 15 foot by 15 foot and located on the top of the hill in the middle of the plantation. From the hut, one could see the small villages scattered along the coast, the sea waves breaking on rocks and beaches, and the endless horizon of the vast Pacific Ocean. The top wooden floor, raised about 10 feet high, was used for sleeping and the ground dirt floor was for eating, cooking and storage for all sorts of things. Surrounding the hut were pawpaw trees, avocado trees, and taro and ta'amu plants.

"What are we eating tonight, Grandma?"

"We are going to have a barbeque", Grandma replied. She then ordered Tusi to go and collect some of the spiny branches of the anoso plant growing about 50 metres from their small hut, and then climb the pawpaw tree using the wooden ladder and tie the spiny branches at the base of pawpaw leaves covering the pawpaw fruits.

"Why do we do this Grandma?"

"We are preparing ourselves for the flying fox game. Very soon in the evening, the hungry flying foxes will come in to feed on the ripe pawpaw fruits. As they dive in, their wings will be caught in the spines and they won't be able to get out again."

"Okay, so then what do we do?"

"Then all we have to do is to kill the flying foxes we need for our barbeque and leave the rest on the tree for the next time we need them."

"Why don't we kill them all?"

"We don't have a fridge to keep the meat so it is better to leave the bats feeding on the tree and therefore we will have fresh meat any time we want."

"That is smart. I love that Grandma."

"Well that is the kind of game you play on the plantation. You play to catch the creatures that eat our produce. At the same time, we get fresh food for free every day."

As they enjoyed their evening barbeque by the fire, Grandma asked Tusi not to throw away any bones or leave leftovers around the hut to avoid attracting rats. Instead, she instructed him to put all the leftovers into a basket and said they would take them to a special place to keep.

"Okay son, you take the fire (a bundle of dry coconut leaves) and I will take the leftovers."

About 20 metres from the hut was a hole of about one metre by one metre and one and a half metres deep. Grandma placed a few sticks across the top of the hole with a few banana leaves covering the sticks. In the middle of the structure she placed the leftovers.

"Why do you do that Grandma?"

"This is another game we play in the bush, but I will explain tomorrow how to play."

That night as they lay in their mosquito nets, Grandma told Tusi some historical stories and genealogies of different families in Samoa. As they were going to sleep, there was some noise like somebody was uprooting the taro plants, followed by the cracking of dry twigs and leaves, coming from the direction of the hole.

"Grandma, listen, can you hear that?" whispered Tusi.

"Shush, I think we have struck luck tonight."

"What do you mean?"

"I think the barbeque bones have attracted the luck and if that is correct then we will have a great week."

"Grandma, it's like a sound of…"

"Shush, I think we have had a great night", whispered Grandma." Do not worry about it now, Tusi, and try and get some sleep."

Before Grandma woke up, Tusi was awakened by the cries of early birds. He quietly sneaked out from under the mosquito net and looked out over the green plants and trees surrounding the hut. After creeping down the wooden steps to the ground floor, he collected a few small stones for his slingshot. As Tusi fired a few shots at some of the noisy birds swooping in and out of the nearby trees, he heard the squeals of piglets. Quietly, with his slingshot ready to fire at any unsuspecting bird, Tusi waded his way through the taro plants towards the sound of the piglets. As he got closer, Tusi found that the pig cries were coming from the hole where they placed the leftovers the previous night. Quickly, Tusi ran back to alert his grandma.

"Grandma, there are pigs in the hole where we placed the leftovers last night. Come and see", yelled Tusi.

"So, we struck some luck last night. Isn't that great?"

"I don't know but the pigs are in the hole. Where did they come from?"

"They are wild pigs. They normally come at night and eat our taro plants. So, we have to set up traps to catch them."

"That is a great idea."

"Well, that is another kind of game you play in the plantation. You play with the wild pigs. They came to eat your taro while you sleep, and you trap them for food. You play to get food for free. Do you think your friends know how to play this game?"

"Never. All they know is how to mock and tease."

"You see son, your friends spend money on buying *pisupo* and you don't spend a penny to get your barbeque meat and…"

Tusi interrupted her saying, "And we used the leftovers from the barbeque to catch the wild pigs for free, and we have a few bats we can eat anytime for free, and we have a lot of pork from the sow for free, and piglets in the pen for free. Oh yes, that is good, no starving in the bush."

"Yes, I told you that life in the plantation is very pleasant."

As Grandma was explaining to Tusi the details of the trick used to catch the wild pigs, Sole, one of their dogs arrived from the village, and ran straight over and barked at the pigs in the hole. A minute later, Tusi's parents and sisters arrived from their early walk from the village.

"Dad, we caught a few flying foxes and some wild pigs – a sow and two small piglets", said Tusi excitedly.

"That is great. So, what are we going to do with the pigs?"

"Well, Grandma said that we will be killing the sow and cooking it for her birthday today and we are keeping the piglets in a pen for future food."

"Well, you will have to help me with the cooking and…"

"Oh yes, I will help to kill the sow, do the cooking, and build the pen. I will collect the leftovers for our trap tonight after tying some more anoso spiny twigs on the pawpaw leaves", interrupted Tusi offering his help without receiving any instructions.

After a day of eating food to celebrate Grandma's birthday and doing plantation work, Tusi's parents and sisters prepared their loads of food to take with them back to the village.

"Are you coming with us Tusi?" Fi asked.

"No, I am staying with Grandma and will go back on Saturday."

"But your friends will ask about you, especially when they want you to join in with their games."

"Tell them that the games I am playing in the bush are better than the marble shooting we play in the village."

"Why?"

"Because we don't get free food with marble shooting."

Because of his growing interest in the pig trap, Tusi offered to collect any little bit of leftover food and to set up the pig trap.

"Do you think we will have more luck tonight, Grandma?"

"I don't know but it will be great if we do."

After their story telling that night, Grandma and Tusi went to sleep. At dawn, a cracking noise woke up Tusi. The noise came from the direction of the pig trap.

"Grandma, I hear a noise from the trap, so we have some luck", Tusi whispered, pushing the back of his snoring grandma.

"Okay. We will check it later but get some sleep for now", said Grandma before rolling over and going back to sleep.

The cry of early birds woke Tusi again later in the morning. As he got up, he heard a dog cry coming from the direction of the trap. The crying went on for a while and Tusi whispered to Grandma, "Sole has arrived."

"Go and check", said Grandma.

Keen to find out the result of his trapping experience, Tusi climbed out from under the net, picked up his slingshot and down he went to the trap. Getting closer to the trap with his slingshot ready to fire, Tusi was surprised to find, not Sole, but a different dog trapped in the hole. Tusi ran back to alert Grandma.

"Grandma, a different dog is caught in the trap. Come and see."

"I thought so. It must be a stray hunting dog."

Just then, a big man with a beard holding a bush knife appeared through the taro patch. The man was a pig hunter who was following the cry of help from his dog.

"Good morning. I beg your pardon mum for entering your plantation at this early time of the morning. From a distance I heard a dog's cry, so I had to follow to check to see if it is my dog. That is why I am entering your plantation without permission", said the hunter.

Grandma accepted his apology and allowed the hunter to take his dog and leave.

When the hunter had gone Tusi said, "That stupid dog must be very hungry."

"Yes, you are right son. Hungry creatures without food always go and search for something to eat. The hungry bats came looking for our ripe pawpaw, the hungry pigs and the dog were attracted to our nice smelling scraps and therefore were caught in our traps."

"I am glad that I am not like those hungry creatures", declared Tusi.

"Ha ha don't be so quick in saying that, because one day, you may not find any food when you are hungry, and you will end up going in search of food just like those creatures. In that case if you are not careful, you may be attracted to some nice smelling food, if not scraps, and trapped just like the pigs and the dog."

"No Grandma, I don't want to be caught up in any trap."

"Well, in that case you have to work hard in the plantation to make sure you have enough food to eat when you get hungry any time. Because if you don't have food when you get hungry, you will certainly go and look for food. In doing that you will most likely be caught in a trap, just like the hungry dog, bats and pigs."

"No Grandma, when I am hungry, at least I now know how to set up our traps to get food."

"That is a very good thing to learn son. But, don't depend on trapping to satisfy your hunger every day."

"Why not?"

"Because if there are no hungry creatures, your traps would be empty and you will die of starvation", said Grandma. "Do you think those bats and pigs and dog would come to our traps had they been well fed elsewhere?"

"I don't think so."

"Very good answer. So, don't depend on traps for food when you are hungry. The only sure food for your survival is what you plant and raise with your own hands in your own plantation. Food from traps is a bonus not a certainty." Grandma continued, "Remember, the reason why we set up traps was to catch those creatures that damage and eat our food supply. We usually find that the creatures that damage and eat our pawpaw and taros are the creatures that are good food for us, so we enjoy eating them."

"What about the dog?"

"You know very well that we don't eat dogs and dogs don't damage our pawpaw and taros either. Dogs are good helpers to people because they go hunting for the wild pigs but because that dog was hungry, it accidently ended up in our trap."

"We still should have killed that dog because it ate our scraps."

"Son, how can you kill a useful animal just because it ate some scraps you had thrown away? If that dog was ours, I would prefer to feed the dog with scraps and let it hunt for the pigs that damage and eat our taro plants while we sleep and rest at night. And in any case, we can still have the pork meat without the trap because of the dog, while we rest at night."

"Oh, I see, I think you are right. That is a good idea Grandma."

Grandma was a strong believer of the saying in Samoa that 'the offspring of people are fed with words and the offspring of birds are fed with flowers. She raised and disciplined Tusi by words of advice and through constant wise counsel always. Grandma also believed that one's security and survival depend on the work of one's hands. She wouldn't allow anything to pass through the awareness of Tusi without counselling with strict and hard training for self-reliance and sufficiency rather than dependency.

Chapter Two

Starting school and tea jars

On Tusi's first day at school, the first bell rang, and a well-dressed, slim lady shouted, "All new kids, come around here and form two straight lines – one for girls and one for boys."

It took a while for the children to follow the instruction. The new kids looked at each other and stood any which way, thinking they were forming two perfectly straight lines as ordered by the tall thin lady.

"Listen all of you. I am your teacher and my name is Ino. You must listen to what I say and move quickly without any noise when I tell you to do anything from now on, okay?" instructed the lady. None of the kids said anything so Ino repeated herself trying to explain what she had said using a mixture of Samoan and English languages. "Listen kids", Ino shouted and banged an empty tin with a stick, "Anytime I ask you to do anything, you must reply 'Yes teacher' because if you don't you will receive the stick, okay?"

The kids shouted, "Yes teacher."

As she gave her instructions, Tusi thought Ino must have been speaking a different level or type of Samoan language because he had no idea of what 'yes teacher' meant. Noticing Sega, one of the kids who normally mocked him, standing nearby, Tusi turned to ask, "What does ES kisa mean?"

Sega replied, "I don't know, just say it."

So Tusi had to memorise these unknown words and reply as the other kids did because he was afraid to get the stick from Ino if he did not.

Ino shouted again, "Form two straight lines. No noise and quickly."

As soon as she finished giving the order, she walked along in a straight line so that the children could position themselves into two straight lines. During this process several kids, including Tusi, were rather lost.

"Did you hear that?" asked Ino.

After Tusi shouted, "Es Kisa", he turned to his left and pushed Sega in the belly because Sega had shouldered Tusi and shouted, "Es Kika." Tusi thought to himself, "I have the liver to defend myself against Sega who always mocks me for eating *eleni*. I will not allow Sega to bully me as he used to do when his cousins and friends were around."

Ino observed this pushing and shoving between Tusi and Sega and called out, "E'e what is the matter?"

Sega, who was in tears, tried to answer, "Tusi pushed my belly and wanted to punch my mouth."

Ino asked Tusi, who was also in tears, "Is that right Tusi?"

"Sega shouldered me and replied to you in the wrong way, saying my mother's name instead", replied Tusi.

"What did Sega say?"

"Sega said es Kika the name of my mother."

"So, what should Sega say, Tusi?"

"Sega should say es Kisa."

Sega interrupted angrily and shouted at Ino, "But that is why I shouldered Tusi because he shouted the name of my mother, Kisa."

"Sega, so what should Tusi say?"

"Tusi should use the name of his own mother and say Es Kika. He should never mention my mother's name."

"But I am the teacher and my name is Ino, not Kika or Kisa. I, the teacher asked the question not your mothers."

Because both boys were lost, Ino took them into the classroom and spoke to them in simple Samoan language, "Listen very carefully. Both your answers were wrong. The correct word is 'teacher' not the names of your mothers, Kika or Kisa (*Fa'alogo lelei mai oulua. E sese uma lua tali. Ole sa'o o le upu o le teacher ae le o igoa o oulua tina o Kika ma Kisa*). So, do not fight and keep saying the word teacher repetitively then it will gradually become easy. (*Aua la le misa ae to'aga e ta'u le upu teacher aua e faifai lava lelei*)." As an exercise, Ino instructed Tusi and

Sega to repeat the word teacher ten times and then asked the boys, "How is it now?"

Both boys replied, "Easy."

Encouragingly, Ino said, "Good try boys but the best way to learn the correct pronunciation is this. You know in the morning when you bring the tea for the teacher in the jar – you say tea jar."

"Do you mean the teapot – *tipoti*?" asked Tusi.

"Yes, the *tipoti* (the pot or jar for the tea) is another word for tea jar. So, when you go home today tell you mothers you have learnt a new word – teacher, okay?" explained Ino.

Tusi and Sega replied, "Yes tea jar."

Still trying to learn the new word, Sega asked Tusi, "What did the tea jar say?"

Tusi replied, "Ino said that, when we go home, we must tell our mothers to bring a tea jar tomorrow."

After the evening devotion Pau, the father of Tusi asked, "How was your first day at school my son?"

"Oh, it was very good Dad. I learnt a new thing from Ino."

"What is that new thing?" asked Pau with a smile.

"Ino taught us kids to call her tea jar."

Without a clue about what tea jar meant, Pau replied, "That is very good son. I didn't know Ino has another name. So which name are you going to use?"

"Any name, Dad."

"Okay, whichever name you use, make sure you speak politely and with respect at all times."

The next morning, about half an hour before the bell rang for the assembly, Tusi saw Sega with a tea jar, and suddenly remembered his tea jar that his mother had prepared early that morning was still sitting on their food cupboard at home.

After giving his tea jar to Ino, Sega came looking for Tusi. "Why did you tell me that Ino wanted us to bring a tea jar? Ino said you were wrong. You didn't understand or listen carefully – your foolish horse. So where is your tea jar? Can't your family even afford a tea jar?"

Furious at Sega's words, Tusi turned red. He asked himself, "Do I have the liver to punch Sega's mouth? Yes, I do." As Tusi turned around for a fight, Ino called both Tusi and Sega to her room to sort out the difficulty. Given the situation, Ino instructed the boys to tell their parents that she would come to talk with them that night.

Soon after Tusi's family's evening devotion, Ino arrived for her discussion with his parents as had been arranged. She was welcomed and allowed to explain the reason for her visit.

"Thank you, Pau and family, for the opportunity. I am here to clarify two issues. First, I would like to inform you of the good effort Tusi is putting into learning the English language in school. However, because of what happened between Tusi and Sega, I think there was some confusion that needs to be cleared up for the benefit of us all, especially Tusi while he is learning English. So, I will speak directly to Tusi, but I wanted the rest of you to hear what I have to say too."

"Tusi, the English word for the Samoan word *faia'oga* (person who does the teaching) is 'teacher'. The pronunciation of this word 'teacher' is very similar to saying the words 'tea jar' which is another term in the English language for 'teapot'. But instead of saying the words 'tea jar' slowly you have to say, 'tea jar' a little faster and then you would be catching up very well with the correct pronunciation of the word 'teacher'."

"So, shall I bring another tea jar for you tomorrow?" Tusi asked Ino.

"No, you don't have to bring a tea jar or *tipoti* (tea pot) but you can come and see your *faia'oga* (teacher) named Ino", replied Ino laughing. She then continued, "The second thing that I want to mention to you parents of Tusi is that, Tusi and Sega often seem to argue and attempt to fight each other at school. Remember Tusi, fighting is not allowed anytime anywhere by the school."

After thanking Ino for alerting him and the family about Tusi's behaviour in school, Pau apologised to Ino for the problems caused due to the misunderstanding and misinterpretation of the new language by Tusi.

When Ino left, Pau spoke with Tusi, "I am very happy with your learning skills, but I am concerned with your behaviour especially with you fighting other kids. What was the problem between you and Sega?"

Tusi replied, "Dad, Sega always mocks me and that makes me angry, so I want to fight him."

Pau said, "Son, I hope you don't mock other kids too, because if you do then there is no point getting angry when other kids call you names. Do you understand that? Mocking is a weakness of kids with little to no training from their parents. So, if you mock others then you are shaming your parents. When other kids call you names, don't retaliate by calling them names back because that shows you are just as weak as them."

"So, what shall I do Dad?"

"Just close your ears and walk away. Do you understand that?"

Because Tusi feared the belt he replied, "I do understand, Dad."

Chapter Three

The Circumcision Saga

One Saturday morning, Tusi played rugby with some of his friends on the beach. After a little while, Tusi and his friends saw some boys from their village chasing chickens in the small area of shrubs between the beach and the hospital.

One of Tusi's friends shouted, "Hey boys, let's join them."

So, the boys stopped their rugby game, picked up a few sticks and stones and went after the chickens. At the end of the chase they were all exhausted, but they had caught a few hens, chicks and medium-sized roosters.

A big boy named Laki called everybody together and asked, "Now boys, do you know why we needed to catch these chickens?"

The boys who were part of the original group with Laki all shouted, "Yes." On the other hand, Tusi and those who joined the chase from the beach had no idea of the purpose of the chase, so they didn't say much at all.

"In case you do not know," said Laki, "these chickens are for the doctor. Today, we are going to give the doctor the chickens so that we can be circumcised. You know, in our culture, all males must be circumcised. If you decide not to be circumcised in life, you are not a

Samoan and you and your children will always be known by the name – the coward with foreskin. This includes you who have joined from the beach, okay?"

Without a full knowledge of what circumcision was, some of the boys including Tusi all said, "*Ia* (meaning yes)."

Laki shouted, "Okay?"

They all shouted, "*Ia ua lele*i (meaning yes and all right)."

"Listen boys, I haven't finished. When we get to the hospital and the doctor or the nurses ask where you got the chickens from, then you must tell them the chickens came from your homes. If anybody mentions anything about our chicken chase then I and the rest of the group will beat you to death", warned Laki.

Everybody agreed and said "*Ia ua lelei.*"

After going through the circumcision operation, the boys all hobbled back to the sea to bathe their cuts in the seawater as advised by one of the nurses. In order to arrive at home in time for the Saturday evening prayers, they all started walking home well before sunset. Tusi's family and many others from the village were surprised to see a group of boys each with bandage hanging down in front of their legs and who were walking unexpectedly slowly and swaying. People laughed and looked happy and congratulated the bigger boys for taking most of the younger boys through the circumcision process. The families of the boys were so proud, and they called them brave worriers.

People kept congratulating them as they went to church on Sunday morning.

Unfortunately, during the Sunday morning church service, the pastor called upon all the circumcised boys to stand up and come to the front of the congregation. To the surprise of the congregation, the pastor read out a note from one of the orator chiefs of the village where the hospital is located (there are two main types of chiefs or *matai* – *ali'i*, the paramount chief, and *tulafale*, an orator chief who speaks on behalf of the *ali'i*).

The note read: "Dear Reverend Maka, I wish to bring to your attention that a group of boys from your village chased and caught our chickens to take them to pay the doctor for their circumcisions. As this practice is not allowed in the teaching of Jesus Christ, I would like your consideration in warning these boys that their actions deserve the penalty of replacing our chickens as soon as possible. If they fail to do so, I will present the names of these boys to the council of chiefs and suggest that they should be punished for their theft."

Because of the seriousness of the letter, the pastor advised all the parents and families concerned to immediately consider making repayments a soon as possible after church.

After the morning service, Tusi's parents called upon him to explain the situation. They then warned Tusi of the consequences of taking and using other people's property and belongings without their permission. They impressed upon him that as the boys had not sought and gained the permission of the owners of the chickens, what they had done was stealing, which is a practice not allowed by the community or by God. So, the whole event was sinning against God.

Because of Tusi's wound, his father did not give him a hiding but strongly warned him of the impact and severe consequences of freely taking things without the permission of the owner. To resolve the issue and to escape severe punishment from the council of chiefs, Tusi's dad immediately sent Tusi and his mother with one of their hens that was laying eggs on the shelf in their house in repayment for the chicken that had been taken for payment for Tusi's circumcision. Similarly, the parents and families of the other boys involved repaid their fines with chickens almost immediately.

After evening prayers that night, Dad asked Tusi, "Why did you join this circumcision saga?"

Tusi replied, "Dad, I wanted to show the kids I am a brave boy and I did not want any kid to mock me and my family and call me a coward with a foreskin."

Tusi's dad laughed and patted Tusi on his head saying, "There is always a better way of doing things that you don't know but we do know. That is why you must listen to, obey and respect your parents because your ways always end up in shame for your parents, unnecessary waste to your family and disobedience to God. See son, you were thinking about yourself only, and that was why you showed off so that the kids won't mock you. However, in doing that you ignored the shame your parents would bear because you satisfied your wants with a stolen chicken.

Being a circumcised for a young boy is exciting. However, your excitement has become a barrier to closeness with God because you had focused on personal pleasure using stolen chickens. Now we have lost one of our best productive hens as a repayment for the stolen chicken."

"I am sorry Dad", Tusi said. His mother also apologised on Tusi's behalf thinking that his dad would belt Tusi.

"Well son, you won't get the belt tonight, but you have to work hard from now on feeding the chickens so that we get more chickens to replace the hen we spent on your circumcision."

"Thank you, Dad, I will."

When Sega and his cousin Fenika caught up with Tusi in a rugby game a few days later, Sega taunted Tusi, "So, you are one of those boys who stole a chicken for your circumcision, ah?"

Tusi replied, "Sega, we didn't steal but we were misled by the bigger boys. However, you say it, I don't care because we all repaid the chickens. What is important is that we are no longer cowards with a foreskin."

Fenika turned to Sega and said, "Tusi is right, you can't talk like that because we haven't removed our foreskins. At least Tusi had the liver to cut off his foreskin, so just shut up and play the game."

After that incident, Sega started to ease up on mocking Tusi, and Fenika and Tusi became good friends.

Chapter Four

Serving up fish soup

On his way to school one morning, Tusi diverted to the seashore. He took off his *ie lavalava* (wrap around) and placed it on a dry coconut leaf and dug a few crab holes on the sand while awaiting the incoming fishermen returning from their night's fishing. When the small white and grey crabs came out of the holes Tusi dug and scuttled for their lives towards the sea, Tusi would chase them until the crabs disappeared into the sea. When he didn't catch any crabs, Tusi enjoyed bathing and swimming in the warm sea and called out to kids passing by to join him.

As the fishermen came ashore after their night of fishing, Tusi called out hello and quickly made friends. It was almost as if Tusi was especially employed to welcome the fishermen home and compliment them on their hard work at night in the deep ocean. Tusi then helped the fishermen pull their small canoes through the shallows and lift them onto the shore and would willingly offer his *faife'au* (service), without an invitation, to do whatever the fishermen asked him to do.

Tusi offered his help and service to Lata to carry his basket of fish home. Lata lived four homes away from Tusi's home and was a very good friend of Tusi's father. Accepting Tusi's offer, Lata told Tusi to take the basket home and to remind his wife Fia'ai, to hurry the cooking because Lata was very hungry. Without any delay, Tusi picked up the basket of fish and sang as he headed to Lata's home. Ahead along the way, Tusi saw a few people from the village including the village *faife'au* (pastor) waiting for the only truck to take their copra to sell to the store in the next village. Tusi circled around to avoid them, as he knew they would tell his father that he had skipped school.

Arriving at the home of Lata, Tusi introduced himself to Fia'ai, "Here is a basket of fish from your husband Lata. He told me to give this to you and to tell you he is very hungry. I could help you with speeding up the cooking."

"Thank you so much Tusi. Are you sure you want to stay and help and *faife'au* (do the service)?" asked Fia'ai.

"Definitely. I like doing whatever you want me to do", Tusi replied.

"What about school today?" Fia'ai asked.

Tusi replied, "Well, I am not feeling well for school today. I will go tomorrow."

Fia'ai quickly wrapped two large fish in a breadfruit leaf and told Tusi to go and take the two fish for the *faife'au* (pastor). (In the culture of Samoa, the pastor is considered a representative of God in the community. As sign of respecting God, the best of everything is given to the faife'au).

Tusi ran off with the fish and was back within five minutes.

"That was quick, where did you put the fish?"

"I put them in the basket and hung the basket on the post at the back of the house."

"You're a very good boy Tusi. Well we only have one coconut, but we need more for the cooking. Can you run to our coconut plantation (which was about five minutes away), to collect another four coconuts for our *suai'a* (fish soup) and *ota* (raw fish) while I start doing the cooking?" asked Fia'ai.

Without any hesitation Tusi responded, "Yes and okay." Running to fetch the coconuts was a big job to Tusi but he had to go as he was hungry too. As he ran, Tusi remembered his father putting aside some of their coconuts in their cooking hut to feed their pigs and chickens in the evening. So, instead of going to the plantation, Tusi took the short cut to his own house and collected four of his father's coconuts and hurried back to the home of Fia'ai.

"Waoooo that is very quick Tusi, you are really a good helper and your service is brilliant and efficient. Your parents must be very proud of you, ah? I wish my boys Sone and Sua would be as good as you. Keep up the good work", complimented Fia'ai.

After assisting with the cooking, Tusi helped Fia'ai to serve the food for chief Lata. When Lata finished eating, Fia'ai invited Tusi to eat together with her because she was very happy with Tusi's service (according to the culture of Samoa, children normally eat after serving the parents and adults).

"Thank you", replied Tusi as he joined her.

After lunch, Tusi joined two other kids, who were shooting marbles near chief Lata's cooking house. They enjoyed the game because nobody was a big looser throughout.

Later in their game, Sita asked Tusi, "What were you doing in Fia'ai's house?"

"I was helping with the cooking", replied Tusi.

"And you stayed and ate with the family, ah?" asked Sita.

"Well, Fia'ai invited me to eat with them because I was doing good service. What is wrong with that?" replied Tusi.

"Nothing wrong but we know that you always eat in any family you go to because your poor family doesn't have enough food", mocked Sita.

"I beg your pardon. What did you say? Boy we have a lot of food. But when I go to other families, I do help them and serve the people of those families and that is why they give me food and, in that case, it is none of your business at all, okay?" Tusi answered angrily.

Pua, Tusi's eldest sister, was walking home from school when from a distance she saw Tusi pushing and shoving with Sita. She called out, "Tusi what are you doing there? Come on, it is time to go home."

With Pua's timely intervention stopping the fight between the boys, Tusi shouted, "Keep going Pua, I will catch up with you."

Pua went home, threw her exercise books on the box where her mother kept all their clothes, opened their wooden cupboard where they kept their Bibles, hymn books, sugar and salt, and found nothing there to eat. She rushed to the basket hanging on the post (where her mother normally keeps the leftover food) and found half a breadfruit, three small taros and two large raw fish wrapped in a breadfruit leaf.

Tusi arrived home to see Pua standing by the post at the back of their house eating a piece of breadfruit and trying to figure out where the raw fish come from. She thought to herself, "Poor Dad he must have gone fishing last night and caught these beautiful big fish. He probably forgot to put the fish in the food safe before going to the plantation early this morning." Seeing Tusi, Pua asked, "Tusi, did Dad go fishing last night?"

"I don't know. Why?"

"There are two beautiful large raw fish in the basket, and I wondered where they came from?"

"Oh no, they are from Fia'ai the wife of chief Lata, a very good friend of Dad."

"Why did she give us fish?"

"Well I was helping to *faife'au* (do the work) of Lata and Fia'ai this morning. I helped Lata lift his canoe onto the shore, take his basket of fish home, and then helped Fia'ai with her cooking and setting the meal for chief Lata. Because of my help and as I was willing to stay and *faife'au* (do the service) for them, Fia'ai gave me the two big fish and sent me to deliver the fish to our home first before we did the cooking."

"Tusi, that was very good work. I am proud of you brother. Helping people to do their work always pays off, ah? Well go and change into your *ie lavalava* (working clothes), have something to eat, breadfruit or taro, and have a short rest. Then you can help me cook a fish soup for our meal tonight so it will be ready when Mum and Dad return from the plantation."

After the evening devotion, Pau, in giving his word of advice and counselling, as usual reminded his children about the importance of listening, obeying, and respect in the Samoan culture. He also emphasised the significance of helping other people through any service possible. Then Pau told the children to get the food ready, as it has been a long day and he assumed everybody would be hungry.

"What is for dinner tonight?" asked Dad.

"We have breadfruit and *fa'alifu* (taro boiled in coconut cream) and *suai'a* (fish soup)", replied Pua.

"Where did you get the fish?" Dad asked.

"Well, Tusi was helping to *faife'au* (do work) for the family of Fia'ai and Lata and Fia'ai gave him two very nice fish to bring home", answered Pua.

"That was very good service son. Did you thank the family, Tusi?" asked Dad.

"Oh yes, Dad. Lata caught so many nice fish and they had a lot left over", explained Tusi.

"That was a very good example of helping people in any service possible, thank you my son", added Mother.

"Okay, prepare a plate of food for the *Fa'afeagaiga* (a polite word in the Samoan language for pastor or faife'au) and *faletua* (a polite word for the wife of the pastor or to'alua). Take the other whole fish and a plate of taro. Tusi, you can go and deliver the food for the *Fa'afeagaiga* while you girls set out our mats of food", ordered Pau.

At the pastor's house, Tusi sat down at the back of the house and spoke using the polite language his father had taught him, "*Fa'afeagaiga* and *faletua* (Reverend and wife), here is a plate of food from my parents."

"Thank you so much. God bless your family and send our love to your parents and the girls", replied the pastor and his wife.

In a short while Tusi returned home, sat down by the back post of their *fale* (house) and said, "Dad and Mum, the pastor and his wife conveyed their big thank you for the food, and they also send their love to you and the girls."

"Good on you Tusi", said his parents.

In the Samoan culture the parents eat first while the children do the serving. The fish soup was so nice that Tusi's parents finished the fish leaving the soup for the children. Tusi's parents then pushed forward their mat of leftovers indicating they had finished eating.

"Thanks to God for the food and thanks to you children for the service", said Tusi's parents.

Tusi removed the food mat while Fi provided a washing bowl and hand towel for their parents. Because there was no more fish left, Dad told Pua to get one of the tins of *eleni* from their food safe to share amongst them, in addition to the fish soup. The children enjoyed their meal while joking and laughing with their parents.

In the middle of the children's meal, Fia'ai and her son Sone arrived. They entered through the back and sat down by the children. They had brought with them a small pot of fish soup including four fish. Once they had settled down Fia'ai spoke, "Pau and Kika and children, here is a pot of fish soup from Lata. We knew that nobody from your family went fishing because you parents were working on the plantation and the children went to school, so my husband asked me and Sone to bring this fish soup for your family. He also conveyed a big thank you for the good *faife'au* (service) provided by Tusi. Tusi did the running around today doing this and that for our family because our kids Sone and Sua went to school. Tusi ran and took the two nice fish for the *faife'au* (pastor), and he ran to collect some coconuts. Tusi was a very good boy. We really wish our kids would be like Tusi in helping and serving other people. He was so good in doing the necessary service. If only we had a kid like Tusi we would train him to be a real pastor."

There was a big silence in the house for a while and Pau, suspecting something strange had happened, spoke, "How's Lata and the rest of the family? I wish to thank chief Lata for the hospitality. Thanks to you and the children for bringing the fish soup. May God give many blessings to chief Lata and your whole family. Are you sure you have enough fish soup for your family?"

"Oh yes, there is plenty. Lata is well; he is just lying on his mat stretching his back. Oh yes, we have more than enough. We also sent my other son, Sua, with fish soup for the pastor and his family tonight while we came here to deliver yours, so don't worry we have plenty", replied Fia'ai.

While trying very hard to sort out the information and news of the evening in his mind and piece together what was really happening, Pau told his children to get a mat of food for Fia'ai and Sone but Fia'ai declined saying they had just finished their meal. Pau offered a cup of cocoa but Fia'ai also refused. As a sign of respect in the culture of Samoa, the children of Pau stopped eating when Fia'ai and her son came into the house. They packed their leftovers and waited to continue eating after the unexpected visitors left.

Soon afterwards, Sua, the second son of Fia'ai also arrived at the back door. Sua had gone to deliver the fish soup for the pastor, only to find the pastor and his wife were already enjoying fish soup brought by Tusi. Because the pastor had a lot of food from other families of the village, they had run out of containers to store any more soup. So, the pastor's wife asked Sua to take the fish soup to the family of Tusi and inform them that the fish soup was from the pastor and his wife because the *faife'au* had run out of storage containers.

When he arrived, Sua's mother and brother Sone were still there talking with Pau and his wife and children so Sua sat down in the space between his brother and the children of Pau. Sua said, "Pau and Kika, this is a fish soup from the pastor and his wife. The pastor's wife said you could make use of this fish soup because they already had the fish soup that Tusi brought tonight."

Suddenly Fia'ai interrupted, "Oh, did you have some fish soup tonight or just the tin of fish? Where did you get your fish? Pau did you go fishing last night. What time did you go because I saw you coming home with your load of taro just before the evening devotions tonight?"

Meanwhile, Pau still did not really know the details of what had and was happening. Instead of directly responding to Fia'ai's questions, Pau was more concerned by the fact that the pastor had exchanged the fish soup they had given him with another fish soup knowingly provided by Lata and his family. Pau spoke, "Oh thanks to the *Fa'afeagaiga* and *faletua*. May God bless the preaching of his word by the pastor and his wife. Thank you very much, Sua. You spoke like a well-trained adult and orated like your father. God bless your schooling and your brother Sone."

Suspecting something was wrong, Kika tried to steer the topic of conversation away from fish soup, "Fia'ai and boys, our children have prepared a basket of pawpaw, ripe bananas, cucumber, and Chinese cabbages and another basket containing taros and breadfruits for chief Lata and your family. This is nothing compared to your love to us parents and the children not only with the fish soup but all other things. As we all believe that it is not what we give you or what you bring for us but the sharing of whatever we get is the practical sign of love and peace amongst our families and the village. The kids will come and deliver these baskets to your home tonight."

Pau added, "Yes Fia'ai, we are so overwhelmed with your hospitality tonight. We are aware that chief Lata is an heir of the king and he does what kings do in helping people. So please convey to chief Lata our sincere thanks. We pray that God will reward and pay back whatever has been lost because of your generosity to us. We pray that God will abundantly provide whatever is required in life to chief Lata, you and the whole family."

Fia'ai thanked Pau and Kika and the children for the token. Then she said farewell and left with her two boys. The children of Pau went along taking the two baskets of food. When the children of Pau returned home, they unwrapped their leftovers and continued eating while Pau and Kika lay on their stomachs facing each other engaged in serious discussion. Pau told his children to eat the *suai'a* that Fia'ai and her son Sone had brought but to safely keep the *suai'a* from the pastor in the cupboard.

After their meal, Pau called the kids together, "Children, while we had enjoyed our food tonight, your mother and I, are quite concerned because there must be a reason why we suddenly ended up with so much fish soup. In our discussion, we tend to believe, based on the information we heard tonight, that the unexpected exchange of fish soup tonight was due to some misunderstanding by Tusi. This misunderstanding has to be explained and sorted out so that you children fully understand the consequences of misunderstanding, regardless of whatever work or service you would do in our family or the community."

Pau looked at Tusi and asked, "Now, Tusi, what is the name of our *Fa'afeagaiga* (pastor)?"

"Maka", replied Tusi.

"What is the name of our *faife'au* (pastor)?" asked Pau.

"That is my sisters and me, Dad, because we *faife'au* (do the service)", answered Tusi and everybody laughed and were amazed as they realised what had happened.

"Okay, this is where the problem started. Tusi please understand that the other Samoan word for the *Fa'afeagaiga* is *faife'au*. *Fa'afeagaiga* is the polite word and *faife'au* is an everyday word. *Fia'ai* sent you to take the two-best fish from Lata's catch to the *faife'au* or *Fa'afeagaiga*, named Maka", explained Pau.

"But Dad, I was doing the *faife'au* (service) not the *Fa'afeagaiga* (pastor)", replied Tusi.

"Okay, Tusi that is true, Maka didn't do the cooking, you and Fia'ai did. Because of your service you were invited to eat lunch at the house of Lata, and we received the *suai'a* tonight as a reward. However, in our culture, *Fa'afeagaiga* Maka is looked upon as the representative of God doing a special service for God. To respect God in our culture we practice giving to God by giving the first and best portion of any harvest to the *Fa'afeagaiga*, okay? So, what Fia'ai instructed you to do was first, to go and take the two-best fish of the harvest of Lata's fishing for Maka who is the *Fa'afeagaiga* or the *faife'au* of our village before you did the cooking. Do you understand that Tusi?" asked Pau.

"Yes Dad, so I was wrong ah Dad? Oh, I am sorry. No, I wasn't wrong – I didn't understand – Fia'ai should have said the name 'Maka', the *faife'au*, because I am also a *faife'au* of our family and I was a *faife'au* in their family. Anyway, I'm sorry Dad for my misunderstanding", apologised Tusi.

Pau took Tusi with him to the house of chief Lata and apologised for Tusi's misunderstanding. After a discussion between Pau and chief Lata, Pau asked Tusi to say a word.

"Please forgive me for misunderstanding Lata and Fia'ai and the children", apologised Tusi.

Lata accepted the apology and commented that Tusi should be taken to Bible school because Tusi already demonstrated good *faife'au* (service) to be a good *faife'au* (pastor).

Feeling guilty about eating the fish that was allocated as an offering for the *Fa'afeagaiga*, Pau believed that he and his wife should also apologise to the *Fa'afeagaiga*. There was a superstitious belief held by Pau and his wife that eating something that was offered for the representative of God would bring suffering to their family in the future.

Taking with them an *ietoga* (a fine mat – a special traditional mat in the culture of Samoa for special events including seeking forgiveness for wrongdoing), Pau and Kika went to apologise to the *Fa'afeagaiga* for their wrongdoing. They explained to the *Fa'afeagaiga* and his wife that their wrongdoing originated from Tusi's misunderstanding of the words spoken to him.

In response, the pastor said, "The service Tusi was doing, that is, helping and serving the people in need, is the same kind of service that I do as the pastor. In that case, Tusi too deserves respect and the best of everything, like the fish he was supposed to bring to me."

Before Pastor Maka closed their fellowship with Pau and Kika with a prayer, he encouraged Pau and Kika to educate Tusi through a church school for Pastor Maka thought Tusi had potential to be a good pastor in the future.

Hearing the news about the fish soup, Lei and her cousin Sega started mocking Tusi, "Sone and Sua told us that you were a very good cook for their family. That is a very good way of getting food, hey pastor. You cook their food and you stay and eat their food, hey pastor. So, pastor, when are you cooking for us? We will make sure we pay you with some *pisupo* instead of fish."

Weighing up in his mind his strong desire to respond with his fists against the very real threat of a belt from his dad, Tusi closed his ears, ignored their words, laughed and walked away.

"Come on pastor, tell us, when are you coming to serve us, your congregation?" shouted Lei and Sega.

Turning his head as he walked away Tusi replied, "One of these days. Bye."

Chapter Five

The mango trap

Lei learned that her cousin Sega always cried and got beaten when fighting Tusi. This made Lei feel so disgusted with Tusi, especially as she kept recalling the unforgettable day when Tusi snatched her ripe banana and ran for his life home. So, Lei waited for an opportunity to pay back Tusi.

One day at school during the break time, the kids were playing hide and seek. Lei selected Sega and Tusi for her team. For hiding places, kids hid under shrubs and up trees around the school ground, and the rugby goal post was used as the home base for the hiding team. During the first round of hiding for Lei's team, Lei and Sega came across a mango tree belonging to a family just outside the school compound. The tree was about 15 metres high and was not easy to climb. Hanging from one of the branches, Lei and Sega spotted four ripe mangoes. Lei and Sega were hungry. The only way to get the fruit was to climb the tree which both could do. Unfortunately, there was a small timber nailed to the trunk of the tree with a warning, newly painted in red, 'Danger – don't climb'.

"Lei, what shall we do? I am hungry and I can't climb because of the cuts on my foot so shall we stone the fruits?" asked Sega.

"Sega, we can't throw stones at the mangoes because the other kids are hiding in the trees on the other side. Where is your friend Tusi?"

"He must be hiding somewhere with Lui."

"Okay, I know what to do", said Lei. "In the next round of hiding we will get Tusi to come with us and get him to climb because he would love to eat a mango. We will get him to give us the fruit while he is up the tree. Then, if somebody comes, we can run away with the mangoes leaving Tusi in the tree. So, we can eat the mangoes and we can blame Tusi for he would be caught up the tree, okay?"

"What about the warning notice on the piece of timber?"

"Don't worry I am going to remove the timber and hide it underneath these dead leaves. Your job is to make sure Tusi comes with us in the next round of hiding."

Using a stone, Lei removed the piece of timber from the tree trunk and asked Sega to collect a few more leaves to ensure it was covered and hidden from sight. Then Sega went and found Tusi and told him about the mangoes.

"Is it a tall tree?" asked Tusi.

"No."

"Is it easy to climb?"

"Well, Lei removed the timber that was nailed across the trunk to make it easier to climb."

Near the home base of the game, Lei also approached Tusi. As bait to attract Tusi, Lei promised that she would make sure the only people sharing the mangoes would be the three of them.

In the next hiding round Lei took Sega and Tusi to the mango tree. They stood there admiring the four ripe fruits that they could clearly identify from the ground.

"Okay, when we get the mangoes, Tusi can take two and Sega and I will have one each", said Lei.

"What if Sega climbs the tree, then he can have two and you and I can have one each?" Tusi suggested.

Lei disagreed, "No Tusi, Sega can't climb because he had cuts on his foot. Also, you can do it much quicker than Sega. Remember, we have to get those mangoes during this round of hiding or Isu and Kone will take them."

"Nnnnn, but you will run away with the fruit before I come down", said Tusi.

"Okay, here is what you can do. When you get up there, you pocket two of the mangoes in your *ie lavalava* to make sure you have your share and throw the other two down to us, okay?" said Lei.

Tusi climbed through the leafy branches and managed to collect and pocket the first mango. He moved up further and collected the second fruit. Because the second mango was nice and ripe, Tusi started eating it as Lei and Sega waited below. With saliva flowing out of their mouths, Lei and Sega longed to get their teeth into their share. While eating, Tusi found another ripe mango in the canopy. This third fruit was more than half eaten by the flying foxes, so Tusi decided to give it to Lei. Through the leaves of the tree Tusi saw Lei. "Lei where are you?" Tusi called.

"I am here", replied Lei.

"Okay, move to your right so that I can see you clearly. Catch your fruit. Don't drop it", commanded Tusi as Lei held tight to the end of her skirt to catch the mango.

"Tusi this is not a good fruit. It is almost completely eaten by a flying fox", called Lei, while checking to see that one of the fruits Tusi was aiming for was still hanging on the tree.

"Lei all the mangoes up here are more than half eaten by the bats. They all look nice from down there. But girl, the bats had a good feed on them probably very early this morning or just before we came."

Tusi then called Sega, "Where are you Sega?"

"Look this way Tusi, I am here on the left of the trunk."

With a bit of flesh left on the seed of the mango he was eating Tusi decided he would give the rest to Sega. "Okay Sega my friend, catch your mango. Make sure you don't drop it."

Sega responded by thanking Tusi as he flattened his *ie lavalava* to catch the mango. Enthusiastically, Lei asked Sega, "Do you have a good or a full fruit? Let me see?"

In an angry voice Lei called, "Tusi you are eating the flesh of the fruits before you give us the seed. See, a flying fox has not eaten this. It is you Tusi, your teeth not the bats – you are a liar Tusi."

Tusi replied with a mouth full because he was eating one of the last two mangoes, "Lei, I am trying to bite away the pieces that were eaten by the bats and then throw the rest of the good part to you." After enjoying about 90 per cent of the flesh Tusi called out, "Lei where are you now? Move near the trunk so you can see me clearly, See this mango?" Tusi showed the seed with a bit of flesh left on it to Lei, "Okay check this one. It is not as bad as your first one, catch, and make sure you don't drop it."

Using her skirt again, Lei caught the mango. It only took a bite to finish what flesh was left over on the seed from Tusi.

When Lei looked to check for the mangoes they had first seen on the top of the tree, she found that all the ripe mangoes had gone. But because she was very hungry, she called out, "Tusi I can see that you are still enjoying eating up there while we haven't had a good fruit as yet, how many more are left Tusi?"

"Lei, I am trying to bite away the pieces of this last mango that were eaten by the bat – do you want the rest of it? There is still a bit on the seed if you want." As Tusi rearranged himself and held tight to the branch, the last mango seed that he was eating fell and hit Lei's arm and the full fruit that he had pocketed in his *ie lavalava* fell and hit Sega's head, making him cry.

Fiercely Lei called, "Tusi you are an idiot. See what you did? Don't you have eyes? Are you a stupid fool?"

Knowing that Lei was very angry, Tusi replied, "Sorry Lei. Sorry Sega. I didn't mean to drop the mango on you."

"Tusi. You are a liar, a stupid liar", shouted Lei as she picked up the full mango that had hit Sega's head. "See, you were pocketing the good fruit, eating the good fruit, and then throwing down the seeds for us ah?"

Tusi replied, "I pocketed that full fruit so that when I come down all of us can share it."

Because Sega was crying and Lei was very angry, Lei picked up the mango seeds and threw them at Tusi, missing him but hitting leaves and branches around him, "Come down, come down, I will punch your mouth when you come down." As Lei kept throwing seeds and hitting the leaves above the branch Tusi was sitting on, hundreds of honeybees emerged swarming all over the place in increasing numbers.

"No, no, no – bees, bees, bees – please stop, please, oh no, Lei, bees, please stop", begged Tusi. When they ran out of seeds to throw at Tusi, Lei picked up the timber with the sign that she had hidden under the dry leaves to look for more seeds. In doing so her fingers were covered in wet, red paint, so she wiped her hands on her skirt and passed the sign to Sega. Finding more seeds, she kept throwing them at Tusi.

"Lei look at this, the sign says, 'Bees on top' – look", said Sega as he wiped his paint-covered fingers on his *ie lavalava*.

"Sega give me the timber, let me see." Lei turned the timber over and read: 'Danger – don't climb' and turned it back again to read: 'Bees on top'. "Okay, let me throw this last seed at Tusi and then we run for our lives." At the same time, the bees also overtook Sega and Lei. "Run, Sega, run", ordered Lei as she fled.

"Please Lei, wait, I am coming down. I am coming down. Wait", begged Tusi as the bees stormed his entire body. As quickly as he could, Tusi scrambled down the trunk, still covered with bees. By the time Tusi hit the ground both Lei and Sega had disappeared. A short time later, Lei and Sega came back with some other kids and helped lead Tusi to the school ground because the whole of Tusi's body was swollen and sore and he could hardly open his eyes.

"What is the matter? Look at that! Why are you so swollen Tusi?" the teacher asked.

"We were stung by a group of bees when we played hide and seek", replied Lei. Given the seriousness of the bee attack, the teacher took

Tusi for a sea bath, believing that the saltwater would remove the poison of the bee sting.

On returning from the sea, Tusi found that chief Salele (who is a relative of Sega and Lei) of the village was at the school complaining to the principal about the children eating his mangoes. The parents of Lei, Sega, and Tusi were also present in response to an urgent request from the principal. Given the news that their children were involved in some event the parents were worried, so they rushed to school. They were very disappointed and angry to find that their kids' bodies were swollen from bee stings, especially in the case of Tusi.

"Dear Tusi, are you all right? Can you see me? How do you feel with your legs and arms, they are so swollen?" asked Tusi's mother.

"I'm okay Mum, my whole body is sore and numb, but I can manage to walk and talk", mumbled Tusi.

"Lei why are your lips swollen, did you fight with Tusi or what happened?" asked Mala the mother of Lei.

"No Mum, the bees stung us when we played hide and seek", replied Lei.

"Thank you all for coming. Our urgent gathering today concerns the complaint of chief Salele about children eating the fruit from his mango tree during the school lunch break today. Apparently, Lei, Sega and Tusi were involved as witnessed from the swollen arms, legs and faces, resulting from the bee stings. While this is sad news to you parents, we must do our job as teachers and make sure the children show good manners not only in school but also in the community. Now, I am going to find out from your children what happened so that chief Salele can then decide about what should be done next. As for the school, we have a policy that whoever causes or initiates problems in the school or between the school and the community, that child would be suspended for a period or for good, depending on the severity of the event. Okay, Lei can you explain what happened?" asked the principal.

"Sega and I saw the mangoes while we were playing hide and seek. We were hungry, and Sega and I could not climb. When Tusi joined us in the second round of hiding, he was also hungry. So, Tusi climbed the tree and Tusi ate the mangoes while sitting on the branch up in the tree, and dropped the seeds to Sega and me", replied Lei.

"Wait Lei, so you and Sega did not eat any of the mangoes?" asked the principal.

"No, we ate only the seeds from Tusi", replied Lei. "And because Tusi dropped the only one full fruit on Sega's head and teased us, we therefore threw the seeds back at Tusi, which disturbed the bees in the hive on the branch where Tusi was sitting and that was why the bees stung all of us, especially Tusi."

"What a selfish kid! Eating the flesh and giving the seeds to my child! Well that child Tusi deserves a punishment because he was selfish to Sega and Lei – terrible manners. He was the one who ate the fruit and therefore he should be the one who should pay – no wonder the bees went for him, selfish idiot", said Mala angrily.

"That is right. Whoever climbed the tree and ate the fruit should pay the price. No person can eat mango seeds because they are hard. Why should my boy get punished if he did not eat any flesh of the mangoes", added Lua the father of Sega?

"Okay, it is time for Sega to explain what happened", said the principal.

"Lei told the truth. We ate the seeds from Tusi and Tusi dropped the full fruit on my head and I cried because it was very painful while the bees stung me", replied Sega with his eyes steadily fixed on Lei.

"So, where is the full mango that hit your head?" asked chief Salele.

"I have it", replied Lei, taking the fruit from her bundle of flowers and handing it to the chief.

Looking at the ripe fruit the chief spoke, "I was reserving about four nice mangoes on the tree, waiting until they were ripe before I picked them to give as my offering to the pastor. Well, at least I can still give the pastor this full fruit.

"Don't tell me that Tusi ate three mangoes that were reserved for the pastor by the chief? That is even worse behaviour and Tusi deserves a serious punishment", complained the mother of Lei.

"You are right Mala. I support what you say because this sort of behaviour is against the culture of Samoa. Anything that was reserved for the pastor is a sacred thing and it should never be touched or used by anybody because besides a heavy fine from the council of chiefs that person will lose his teeth very easily during his life", added Ote the mother of Sega.

"Okay Tusi. It is your turn to explain what happened", said the principal.

While the parents of Tusi were keeping their cool they were quite disturbed because of the blame that was resting on Tusi so far. On the other hand, despite their anger, the parents of Lei and Sega looked relieved given the information provided by their children. Because it took a while for Tusi to say anything, Sega's mother interrupted, "Come on boy, speak. You ate the mangoes, so speak. You threw the full fruit on my son's head, so speak."

Lei's mother also called out, "Yeah boy, tell the true story. Was the mango sweet? What you will be getting will not be sweet but a sour punishment. You will pay for what you did."

Because Tusi was still quiet, the principal asked him again, "Tusi, you have to say something, or we will make the decision based on the information given by Lei and Sega."

While Tusi wiped the tears from his swollen eyes, his mother spoke, "Son, please, tell the true story. Don't worry about the punishment. If the council of chiefs issues a fine, we will bear that immediately to make sure you will be back at school as early as possible."

The principal spoke again, "Tusi are you going to say anything, or shall we make the decision now?"

Nodding his head, Tusi started speaking very slowly and quietly, "Nnnnn, I am sorry chief Salele. Nnnnn, I am sorry principal. Nnnnn, I am sorry to you parents of Lei and Sega. Nnnnnn, I am sorry to you my parents. Nnnnn, I already said I was sorry to you Lei and Sega. In the first place, I didn't know anything about the mangoes until Sega and Lei persuaded me to come and see the fruit on the tree. I didn't want to climb the tree, but Lei and Sega asked me to climb up to pick the four mangoes we identified from the ground. As payment for my climbing services, Lei told me to pocket two mangoes in my *ie lavalava* and throw the other two down to them. When I got up to the branch where the mangoes were, I found that all the mangoes, but one, were more than half eaten by the flying foxes. I then bit away from the fruit the flesh that was eaten by the bats and threw the rest, mostly the seed, down to Lei and Sega. I pocketed the one full fruit in my *ie lavalava* so that when I came down, I could share it with Lei and Sega."

Tusi kept wiping tears from his swollen face as he spoke. Everybody else was quiet. "Because Lei was mistakenly very angry, thinking I was eating the flesh of the fruits and giving them only the seeds, she then threw the seeds at me unnecessarily. The seeds hit the very big beehive that was on the branch near where I was sitting. Because I was trying to save myself from the bees, the full fruit that I had pocketed fell and hit the head of Sega. I didn't throw the full fruit on Sega's head and I couldn't stop the falling fruit because I was clinging to the branch covered with bees. As Lei kept throwing the seeds, I begged Lei not to throw the seeds because the more seeds she threw, the more bees stung me. In lots of pain and with bees swarming all over me, I hurried down while Lei threatened to punch my mouth when I got down. When I finally got to the ground, Lei and Sega had already fled leaving me alone at the base of the mango tree covered with bees.

"Ha ha, so how many full mangoes did you eat Tusi?" asked chief Salele.

"None, chief Salele, I was biting away the parts of the fruit where the bats had eaten them and threw the leftovers with good flesh still on the seeds down to Lei and Sega." Wiping tears from his eyes Tusi continued, "Chief, I did the hard work of service – that is climbing and biting away the bat-eaten parts of the mangoes – while Lei and Sega were enjoying sucking the seeds. I hope I don't get any germs and or a deadly disease from the flying foxes as I already have a swollen body from the poison of the bee stings."

The listeners were speechless. They looked everywhere wondering what to say. The principal nodded his head showing some signs of doubt about the truth of the matter. At the same time, he looked with some pity at the swollen body of Tusi. He was somewhat concerned about the chance of Tusi getting sick because of germs transmitted from the flying foxes, not to mention the seriousness of the poison of the bee stings. "Thank you Tusi, I wondered why your stings were a lot worse than Lei and Sega. Okay, chief Salele what would you say?" asked the principal.

"I understand what the kids were saying about who ate and who didn't eat, and it is very sad to find that the kids were stung by the bees. However, this should not have happened had they obeyed the warning that I painted in red this morning on a piece of timber that I nailed on the trunk of the tree. On one side of the timber I clearly wrote with red paint early this morning: 'Danger – don't climb' and on the other side I wrote: 'Bees on top'. I nailed this timber on the trunk of the tree to warn people that they should not climb to the mangoes because the bees were at the top. When I came around this morning after I heard the kids crying, the timber was lying on the ground", explained Salele.

Because of her anger about how Tusi had treated her daughter Lei, Mala, interrupted again, "You see, Tusi has done a lot of damage this morning. He removed the timber with the warning sign. He ignored the warning sign, he climbed the tree, and he ate the fruit and gave our children the seeds. So, I think he deserves punishment from the school and from the council of chiefs."

Ote the mother of Sega added, "Tusi you said you didn't want to climb so why did you climb a tree with a sign that said don't climb. If you catch any germs from the flying foxes, it's your fault because Lei and Sega didn't tell you to bite away the flesh eaten by the bats. Look boy, don't make excuses after eating the flesh and giving the seeds to our kids – do you think our kids are pigs eating seeds – just watch out boy."

"Okay, calm down ladies. I believe the main cause of the problem rests with the removing and ignoring of the warning sign that was put up by chief Salele. That by itself is a serious offence according to the council of chiefs – isn't that true Salele?" said Pito the father of Lei.

"That is exactly right Pito. Eating the mangoes is not really a serious issue and we may waive a penalty but removing the sign and ignoring the warning are worse offences and will surely warrant a heavy penalty from the council of chiefs. For your information, offences like the removal of the warning sign would normally result in a fine of about eight to ten roasted pigs and 200 taros to the council of chiefs. Similarly, the offence of disobeying the warning sign may pick up another fine of eight to ten roasted pigs and 200 taros. So, in total the matter of concern this morning is not a cheap one to any family in our community", replied chief Salele as Tusi slowly raised his hand.

Hearing the severity of the fine, the parents of Lei and Sega were even more determined to place the blame firmly onto Tusi so that Tusi's family would bear the heavy fine from the school and the council of chiefs.

"Put your hand down, Tusi. The warning said 'Danger – don't climb' and you climbed, not Lei or Sega. Therefore, you disobeyed the order of the chief, so you were wrong and therefore should be punished", claimed the mother of Lei.

"Please principal, the kids have already explained what happened, and it is clear to us all that Tusi caused the problem. Tusi is just making excuses, so why not let chief Salele just tell us his final decision and we can go home. I can't stand looking at Tusi telling lies", complained Ote.

Ignoring Tusi's raised hand the principal continued, "Okay, what is your view so far, chief?"

"Thank you, principal and parents. Given the explanation from the children, so far, I think I will report the matter to be further considered by the council. However, in my opinion, based on the information from the children, I tend to believe Tusi will bear the punishment for disobeying the warning sign. I think, it is now clear that it was Tusi who ignored the warning sign, and climbed, hence causing the disappearance of the mangoes from the tree", said Salele.

The parents of Tusi remained quiet but were furious and disappointed while the parents of Lei and Sega were somewhat relieved and happy with the decision of the chief.

"That sounds like a very fair decision, chief Salele", commented Pito while his wife Mala and, Lua and Ote, the parents of Sega nodded their heads showing their support for the decision.

Without any argument about the case, Tusi's father apologised to chief Salele, the principal, and the parents of Lei and Sega on behalf of his son, and informed the principal and chief Salele that they would prepare to deal with whatever fine would be given by the school and the council of chiefs for Tusi's misbehaviour. Because Tusi was still trying to put his hand up after the apology from his Dad, Pau turned to Tusi and said, "Son, I have already apologised for your misbehaving so don't put up your hand because I think you are trying to say sorry to chief Salele, the principal and the parents of Lei and Sega."

Before summarising the main points of the discussion, the principal asked, "Kids, are you clear now about the final decision of chief Salele or not? Do you have any questions or anything else to say?"

Tusi slowly raised his hand again and nodded.

"Okay, Tusi I know that you were trying to put up your hand before so what is that you have to say?" asked the principal.

"Please chief Salele, what is the fine for lying?" Tusi asked.

"In this case I think the worse fine is another five roasted pigs and 200 taros for the council", answered Salele.

"And the fine for lying is different from the fine for removing the sign and different from the fine for disobeying the sign – is that correct?" asked Tusi.

"Yes", said Salele.

Before Tusi could speak again, the principal inquired, "Tusi, why do you ask that?"

Mala jumped in and said, "Is the fine of lying too much for you Tusi? Yes, that is why you should have told the truth boy."

The principal asked again, "Tusi why did you ask about the fines?"

"Principal, I asked because Lei and Sega should pay all those fines to the council of chiefs", said Tusi.

"Shush Tusi, what do you mean? Didn't you understand the decision of chief Salele? Chief has made his decision already and if you lie then your family may bear another fine", yelled Lei's mother.

Sega's mother joined in, "Look boy, you are not the judge to make the decision. Just speak for yourself, and let the chief make the decision. What were the lies my son and Lei were saying and what more lies are you going to say boy?"

The tension in the room increased. In particular, the parents of Lei and Sega were becoming agitated, while the parents of Tusi were quietly anxious about the potential results of the ongoing discussions.

"Chief Salele and parents, shall we give Tusi a last chance to explain what he really meant please", said the principal.

"Please, Chief Salele, Principal and parents forgive me if in your thinking, I didn't tell the truth about removing the warning sign – only Sega and Lei know that truth. The only truth I know is that Sega and Lei lied to you all. Sega knows who it was who removed the timber with the warning sign that chief Salele nailed on the tree this morning", said Tusi.

Everybody was shocked while the principal turned to Sega and asked, "Sega, you tell the truth – who removed the timber with the sign this morning?"

Looking at Lei and with tears running down his cheeks, Sega said, "Lei removed the timber to make it easier for Tusi to climb the tree."

Principal said, "Oh, so Sega, you saw Lei remove the timber with the warning sign, did you?"

"Yes sir", replied Sega.

"Was Tusi present when Lei removed the sign? Did Tusi know about the timber and the warning sign Sega?" the principal asked.

Sega slowly shook his head side by side.

There was complete silence in the room and a growing sense of anticipation until Tusi slowly spoke again, "Remember, chief Salele and principal and parents that I told you I didn't know anything about any mangoes. During the first round of hiding, Lei and Sega saw the mangoes and during the second round Sega and Lei persuaded me to come and climb. When I went to climb, there was no timber and no warning sign because Lei and Sega had removed it already. Had I found any timber with a warning or sign that said 'Danger – don't climb', I would never have climbed the tree and I would be a fool to give myself over to the enjoyment of the bees if I saw a sign that said 'bees on the top'. In saying that, I certainly respect the decision made by chief Salele and supported by the parents of Lei and Sega – let the guilty person who caused the problem be fined."

A long silent pause ensued. People were looking at each other but saying nothing.

Tusi quietly said again, "Lei and Sega had painted themselves red when they removed the timber. They wiped their fingers on their uniforms as you can see." Tusi pointed to the clothes of Lei and Sega. "The paint on their uniforms tells you chief Salele, principal, and parents the true story of the mango trap."

To break the long silence the principal spoke, "I have nothing else to say because the matter is, I suppose, clearer now. Before giving the time to chief Salele to tell us his final decision I wish to thank each of you parents for coming. I also wish to thank the children for explaining the event. What has happened has happened, and I hope the children have learnt from their mistakes." The principal didn't give any decision on behalf of the school but passed the buck to chief Salele who was now caught on the political fence because of his family relationship with the parents of Lei and Sega, who now seemed to be the ones at fault.

Salele spoke, "I believe this matter should be taken as a warning to you children and us parents. The sign was put in place for a reason. Always read the sign because it will direct you to do the right thing. Given that you all have had some stings from the bees, and I can still give the one full fruit to the pastor, I think I will put an end to this mango issue right here and now. As the principal stated, whatever has happened has happened and I hope the children have learnt from their mistakes."

After their evening meal, Lolo the wife of chief Salele went to the cooking hut to wash dishes and do some cleaning up. At that time Salele remembered the ripe mango he had put aside for the pastor. So tempted by the thought of the sweet juicy fruit he picked up the mango, lay flat on the mat by the front post of the house, and ate the mango while talking to the air, "So sweet, no wonder the kids went for the fruit. Thanks, Tusi. You did a good job by climbing and not eating the only full fruit. You are a very good lad. Lei, you are also a very good girl for hiding the fruit in your flowers so that chief could enjoy what he reserved for him – the pastor will have a fruit next year when the next season comes. Great work kids, nnnnnnyah meeee."

As he enjoyed his mango, Lolo called, "Salele what are you doing? It sounds like you are eating. And who are you talking to?"

Salele replied, "Lolo, I am just biting away the bat-eaten parts of the mango I found under our tree today."

Lolo called with a demanding voice, "You mean the fruit that you reserved for the pastor? Is it sweet? Would you leave a bit for your wife?"

"Well, I don't think I can leave this one for the pastor because it is more than half eaten by the flying foxes. It is very sweet, and of course, I am leaving a bit on the seed for you to taste. It isn't that much but better than nothing."

Lolo rushed over to taste the mango. As she was sucking the juice off the seed, the parents of Lei entered through the back of the house. Swopping the mango seed into her left palm, Lolo shook the hands of Pito and Mala.

"Come, come in, and sit down by Salele", welcomed Lolo as Salele sat up to greet their visitors.

"Sorry for disturbing your meal, I mean your enjoyment of your mango seed Lolo", said Mala.

"Oh no. It's okay. Salele found a very nice fruit that fell from our mango tree today, so I am just tasting the sweetness of the seed. Our tree bears some very sweet fruit. I will bring you a fruit one day", replied Lolo completely unaware of the events of the day.

Overwhelmed by the decision of chief Salele to drop the case, Pito and Mala had come bearing a token of their appreciation, in the form of two *ietoga* (fine mats – a high valued traditional mat is often given in exchange for a favour or to ask for forgiveness in the culture of Samoa), two roast chickens and a basket of cooked taro. Not long after, the parents of Sega also arrived at the house of chief Salele with a roast chicken and a basket of cooked taro as their way of thanking chief Salele for the great decision he had made in dropping the case.

In their discussion, chief Salele advised the parents of Lei and Sega that while he (Salele) had dropped the case, the case was still open to the council unless the principal of the school agreed to ignore the case altogether and providing no other chief would raise the matter to the council meeting.

"Thank you for the token of your appreciation about my decision. Given our blood connection, it was not easy for me to make that decision because as you understood from the information from the kids, Lei and Sega were in fault and you would definitely bear the fine if the case was to go through to the council of chiefs, which according to the policy of the council I should be responsible for reporting it. While I decided to rest the matter, I hope the principal will do likewise by not suspending Lei and Sega", said Salele. "Because if the people of the village know that Lei and Sega were suspended then the case would be reignited and if that occurred, I would need to report it to the council."

"So, what shall we do?" asked Lua, knowing that Salele was skilled in navigating village politics.

"Well you know the culture of our country; you appeal for sympathy. I believe a couple of fine mats, one or two roast chickens, and a suckling pig would be good enough to settle the mind of the principal", answered Salele.

"That is a good idea and I totally support it. However, at this time of the night it is difficult to slaughter and prepare a suckling pig in the dark", replied the mother of Lei.

Salele pictured in his mind a delicious suckling pig which he would have much preferred to roast chickens so he said, "How about you get the suckling pig and bring it to my house tomorrow but for now, take these fine mats, the roast chickens and taros that you brought me and give them to the principal. I also have a case of corned beef to add on top for a better token for the principal. Don't let the principal sleep without something to think about or it may be difficult tomorrow."

Understandably, to take back the things they had brought to chief Salele and give them to the principal was a cultural embarrassment to the parents of Lei and Sega, so the father of Lei said, "Chief, we honour your advice. However, while we believe that the things, we brought tonight will never be enough to counter your brilliant decision today we won't take them back. Respecting your advice, we will prepare whatever we can get tonight for the principal."

"It is all up to you, but if there is any way I can be of help again then just let me know", responded chief Salele.

From experience, the parents of Lei and Sega understood that chief Salele was a very good politician and in some of their family gatherings chief Salele sometimes made up things that weren't completely truthful.

To test the honesty of chief Salele, the father of Lei said, "Oh chief I am sure you can help us in this case."

Chief replied, "Certainly. What is it?"

Pito said, "The shops are closed tonight, is it possible to borrow your case of corned beef and we will replace it tomorrow?"

Chief Salele looked around and spotted his wife at the back of the house. "Lolo can you collect the…"

Lolo became disturbed, "Collect what? Salele, you seem to forget things very easily. Don't you remember that we gave that case as part of our contribution for the funeral of uncle Oti last week?"

"Oh, sorry Pito. It's true. I forgot. Sorry Pito", apologised Salele.

Without delay, the parents of Lei and Sega put together a few fine mats and went to the house of the principal. They begged him to drop the case so that their children would not be suspended. They also promised the principal that they would each provide one live piglet when daylight came. The principal thanked the parents of Lei and Sega for the things they had brought and instead of suspending the children, he asked the parents to keep the children at home for at least one day until their swollen faces got better.

As normal, after the family evening devotion, Pau and Kika discussed the events of the day with their children.

"Tusi I was very concerned at the beginning of the mango eating discussion at school today, especially regarding the issue of you eating the flesh then giving the seeds to Sega and Lei", commented Tusi's mother.

"Mum, you know that I am an enemy of Lei and her relatives? When they asked me to climb, I felt in my heart that they were trying to get me into some trouble somehow. So, I decided to pay myself for doing the work for them regardless of whatever trap they were setting to catch me. They called me a fool again, so I made sure that I was full eating the mango flesh on the tree while they, the real fools, ate almost nothing except for sucking the juice off the seeds", explained Tusi while everybody laughed.

"Tusi, were you nervous when the parents of Lei and Sega accused you or when the chief was about to wrongly penalise you?" asked Pau.

"Dad, I wasn't nervous because I had the liver to speak the truth."

"That was good Tusi. In the beginning of the discussion your mother and I were very nervous because we didn't know whether you were speaking the truth until you proved to everyone what had happened. Speaking the truth was the winning strategy you used to destroy the mango trap, thank you son."

"Dad, is the council of chiefs going to fine the families of Lei and Sega?"

"Son, I don't know but it looks like the chief will not report the matter to the council and I don't know what the principal will do because he hasn't made any decision as yet. But son, whatever will happen it will happen. So, you try and stay away from activities that may cause problems."

"I think they should be fined because if they hadn't removed the warning sign, I wouldn't have climbed, and I wouldn't have been stung by the bees, and I wouldn't get the poison, and I wouldn't get a swollen body", said Tusi who was still fighting the pain from the stings.

"Son, I know how you feel but what good would it do you if the council of chiefs fined the families of Lei and Sega? You may get a tiny piece of pork if you are lucky."

"Tusi, Dad is right, if you don't get anything from the fine why think about it, just ignore it", added Mother.

"Brother do you know how difficult the fine would be to those families. How would you feel, if you were in the wrong and Dad and Mum were fined ten roast pigs and 400 taros? It takes more than five years to raise a pig to the size the council demands. It takes a year to grow the taros. If we were fined, how would we then survive – no, that is too hard, don't you think so?" said Pua.

"No, I still think those families should pay a fine so that their kids won't repeat doing stupid things to me. Yes sister, I don't want any piece of pork, but I want to put a stop to the mocking from Lei and her family and friends."

"My son Tusi, a fine may stop those kids or may cause them to set another trap to catch you as a way of retaliation from the fine – and that would then repeat the unpleasant relationship between you and them repeatedly. However, if you forgive them and be friends with them, then the bad relationship will slowly turn into a good one", advised the mother of Tusi.

In the meanwhile, chief Pulu, who was also the family doctor, had entered the house of Pau. Before Pulu began a conversation with Pau, his attention was drawn to the swelling on the face, arms, and legs of Tusi.

"What's happening, Tusi? Do you have boils again or did you get a hiding from your dad or what? Your entire body is swollen, how come?" asked Pulu.

As Tusi described the events of the day, Pulu grew red scratching his beard, his head and shoulders, and then asked, "So what is the next step? Is Salele going to address the council about the case or not, because if not I will certainly bring it up at the council meeting tomorrow."

Throughout the main part of the council meeting the following day, chief Salele did not mention a word about the mango trap case, even though more than half of the council members had heard about the incident. Some chiefs had also heard that Salele and his wife had accepted the tokens from the parents of the children involved.

When the time came for general matters towards the end of the meeting, chief Pulu courageously started, "I understand that chief Salele has a very important case that needs to be heard and dealt with by this council."

Salele sat up straight, shifted in his seat and moved forward while thinking of how to start. Even though Salele was hoping that the meeting would be over without a mention of the mango case, he was prepared with answers to counter any queries.

"Yes, chief Pulu and the general council, I was waiting for this time to officially inform the council of a very important incident about the three hungry kids eating fruit from my mango tree without my permission. The incident happened yesterday during the school lunch break. Both the principal and I called upon the parents and the kids, and after a very educational discussion, I decided to take the case as a good warning to the kids so that they would learn to be aware and ask permission if they needed anything that does not belong to them. I must inform the council of the fact that the hungry kids did not eat any full fruit because the flying foxes ate most of the fruit. With that brief, I as an owner of the tree, therefore, appeal to the council to please bypass any further discussion of the mango case because the poor hungry kids were not at fault."

Chief Fau, a supporter of Salele thanked Salele for being lenient and considerate with the children and their parents.

The majority of the chiefs showed gestures of appreciation when Fau narrated in favour of Salele but Pulu interrupted again, "Salele could you please explain what you mean because the kids climbed your mango tree to pick the fruit without your permission, which is a misconduct that needs a penalty. And yet you also said that the kids were not at fault. Who, then, was at fault?"

"Thank you for the question. Yes, the kids looked at and admired the mangoes on my tree, removed the warning sign from the trunk, climbed the tree, tasted the bat-eaten fruit, and were stung by the honeybees from the hive on the top of my tree. Yes, they climbed the tree and ate the fruit without my permission. Why? Because they were hungry. Why were the kids hungry? Because the parents, the school, and our village did not provide enough food for the kids during their school meal breaks. Who then is at fault? The kids? No, it is us, the chiefs, because we don't have programs to ensure that the parents, the school, and the whole village provide proper and enough food for our children so that they won't get hungry at meal break times at school. Members of the council, that is why I dropped the case about the hungry kids climbing my tree without my permission. For the same reason, I was tempted to eat the only full fruit left from my mango tree that I had put aside for the pastor – because I was hungry."

There was laughter amongst members of the council meeting.

When Pulu tried to ask another question, Salele continued, "Hunger is a cause of most if not all the problems in our community and yet we either don't see it, think about it, or don't care about it. Hunger is happening everywhere we live, in politics, in sex, in the government and in church. If we are all hungry, then why should we fine the hungry kids?"

"But Salele, the council has guidelines to follow for the security of the community. When you want something that doesn't belong to you then you should ask for permission. In this case, the hungry kids should have asked your permission to climb your tree and pick your mangoes. In addition, you put up a sign showing that you did not permit anybody, including hungry kids, to climb your tree because of the bees, and that sign was removed – again without your permission. Isn't that right Salele?" asked Kota the chairman of the meeting.

"True, chief Kota, but boy when you are hungry, you can almost do anything, including breaking some of the guidelines – the same ultimate reason why the son of Toa eloped with his cousin without the permission of his aunty because he was hungry for sex – the same reason why the politicians design the laws instead of lawyers because the government is hungry for power, etcetera."

There was laughter and clapping around the room in response to Salele's words.

Information had been passed amongst the members of the meeting about special visits by the parents of Lei and Sega with tokens to chief Salele and the principal the previous night. Therefore, some chiefs also questioned the matter of a possible bribe.

"Did you accept any bribe last night Salele?" asked the chairman.

"With due respect to this council, there is a difference between Samoan traditions and a bribe. In our culture, giving thanks is more than the mere words 'thank you *Fa'afetai*'. When we appreciate things, we give more than the words 'thank you *Fa'afetai*'. The parents of Lei and Sega came to my house last night with tokens of their appreciation because it is our tradition. They gave these tokens after, not before, I dropped the case – so it was an extension of their thanksgiving not an inducement for me to drop the case.

The chairman interrupted, "Salele, did you tell the parents in front of the principal that you would drop the case?"

Salele answered, "Yes, chief Kota."

"Don't you think the decision about whether or not to drop the case should be made by the council?" asked Kota.

"Oh yes, of course, Mr Chairman. The parents knew, because I reminded them, that the case would be brought to the attention of the council and this council makes the final decision according to its protocol. However, as far as lodging a complaint to the police, the representative of the government for the application of laws from overseas, I, as an owner of the mango tree, told the children and parents concerned in front of the principal that I had dismissed or dropped the case because that is my personal business."

Further laughter and clapping erupted in the house.

Before the council provided its decision, the chairman asked Tala, the chief of the family of Tusi, "How did the parents of Tusi and your family see the outcome of the mango case?"

"Mr Chairman and the council, while there was no apology from the parents and or the family of the kids, namely Lei and Sega, to the parents of Tusi and our family, the parents of Tusi have asked me to inform the council that they would forgive the kids and their parents, and wouldn't lodge any complaint to the police on any matters about the mango case", replied Tala.

The members were surprised because all were expecting a strong demand for a serious fine, especially for the damaging remarks and wrong accusations directed at Tusi from the parents of Lei and Sega during the discussion.

"Also, Mr Chairman, I, on behalf of the parents of Tusi and my family ask the council for leniency if its decision is to lay a fine on the family of Salele. Additionally, I would like to move that this council should seriously consider better ways to deal with the hunger of children at school as indicated by chief Salele", added Tala.

At the end of their deliberations, the chairman on behalf of the council of chiefs thanked the parents of Tusi through chief Tala, and chief Salele for not presenting the mango trap case to the police. The council of chiefs also thanked chief Salele for alerting them of the issue, and chief Tala for supporting the issue, for the council to consider better communal policies for the problem of hunger in the school. However, because of the plea for leniency from chief Tala and his family, the council of chiefs fined the families of Lei and Sega only two roast pigs and 100 taros, with the condition that the parents of Lei (Pito and Mala) and Sega (Lua and Ote) apologise to the parents of Tusi.

After fulfilling the decision of the council, Pito and Mala called their children, Lei and Fenika, together for a discussion.

Pito spoke, "Lei, why do you always have problems with Tusi?"

"Every time we play together, he always outsmarts us, as if he ..."

Mala interrupted, "Well, he outsmarted you all right – he ate the mango flesh and we paid the fine. That was smart not outsmarting. Look Lei, stop this nonsense of calling names and try and speak the truth all the time. I hope you know now that lying is very expensive; it creates anger unnecessarily; and brings embarrassment not only to you but to our whole family. You see, we were so unnecessarily angry at

Tusi because you didn't tell the full and true story. And, when the truth was told we were so embarrassed, and we had to apologise to his family. Luckily, the family of Tusi accepted our apology or we would be facing more fines resulting from wrong accusations. After all, we believe that Tusi is a smart boy from the way we heard him speak during the investigation. Look girl, if you can't outsmart him then if I were you, I would get closer to him and make him a friend. Who knows, he could be a very good husband for you? He looks good to me."

Pito spoke again, "Please children try and avoid these kinds of problems because our family doesn't have the resources to pay more fines. Secondly, as principal of the district school, I don't want my children to be the cause of unwanted behaviour in the community. I need you to support my job by demonstrating good manners everywhere in the village especially the school. Do you understand that Lei?"

"Yes Dad, and I am very sorry for what has happened", replied Lei.

Chapter Six

Chicken rings and late-night intruders

When he was 14 years of age, Tusi moved up to the district school. There, Tusi's best friends were Fou, son of Pastor Maka, and Fenika, son of Pito, the headmaster of the school. Fou had made friends with Tusi through Fou's sister Susana, known as Su. She loved to share the nice food she brought from home as snacks with Tusi during school meal breaks. Fenika became friends with Tusi through rugby and through his sister Lei, who had once been an enemy of Tusi but after the mango incident they eventually became very close friends.

During Tusi's final year, the school planned a live concert to raise money for a school trip to experience life in some of the Pacific islands including Fiji, Tonga, Niue, and American Samoa on the ships MV Matua and MV Tofua. The teaching staff who made up the management team for the concert, planned to use the concert to select good performers and items for the Pacific trip.

The students learnt and practiced different plays, dances, songs based on the cultures of the Pacific islands. They also prepared costumes and special speeches and orations. Amongst the key actors were Tusi and his friends Fou and Fenika. Because the three boys had similar talents for conducting large choirs, dancing cultural dances, singing and oration, they were heavily involved in the preparation of the concert and the actual performance.

On the night of the main play, Tusi was selected to conduct the *pese o le feiloaiga* (opening song) and the *taualuga* (closing song or item), which were the most important items in the show. Meanwhile, Fou and Fenika were given the responsibility of supervising all other performances during the show. Sieni the adopted sister of Su, whom Tusi liked very much, was the main *taupou* (dancer) featured in the *taualuga*.

At the opening song, Tusi jogged to the front of the stage dressed in his conducting costume. Standing in the middle of the choir, he bowed to the crowd, hit his conducting sticks once, twice, three times and jumped as the beginning note (muao) of the song burst forth from the choir. The singers swayed as they sang, their bodies following the movements as directed and guided by Tusi's hands and legs. Tusi, using his body language and movements matched the ups and downs of the melody. He put on a remarkable display that was talked about by people in the district for some time afterwards. The supreme confidence demonstrated by Tusi at the start of the show encouraged the students to perform to the best of their abilities throughout the rest of the concert. After each item throughout the show, people kept calling out Tusi's name and shouting out requests to bring back items with similar styles as Tusi had displayed in the beginning.

Before Tusi started the *taualuga* (last and closing item), the crowd was clapping and shouting for more and more and kept calling the name of Tusi. When Tusi made a sudden clap, coinciding with a big bang as Fou struck an empty tin, the crowd went quiet. Then the final song started. People remained silent throughout as Tusi entertained and the choir sang, expertly conducted by Tusi. To the amazement of the crowd, at the end of the song Tusi made a stylish high jump and landed on his feet. His conducting *sulu* (wrap around) fell forward covering his head as he bowed to the crowd.

"More, more, Tusi, Tusi, Tusi, more, more, more", shouted the people.

Everybody including the staff and students joined the crowd, standing and clapping to acknowledge the super performance by Tusi while Tusi slowly raised his head, lifted his left hand and waved to the crowd with his fingers dancing in the air. Apart from his thumb, a bright yellow rubber ring encircled each of his fingers. The rings were the rubber rings used by Tusi's father to mark their chickens.

When the play was over and the crowd had disappeared, the staff congratulated the main actresses and actors especially Tusi and Sieni.

"Well done Sieni. I loved your style", complimented Tusi.

"Oh, thanks Tusi. I congratulate you too. You look super and sexy. You did a very good job."

"Girl, I have no words to describe your beauty tonight. I was so surprised."

"Well, that was nothing Tusi but don't worry because one day I will give you a special surprise."

"I'll keep that in mind."

Students complimented each other as they all walked home. Su pushed her way through the crowd and managed to get hold of Tusi's hand. She swung him to face her, hugged him tightly and kissed his neck.

"E'e, Tusi that was something else. That was a super performance. Nobody ever did that kind of thing in our district before", said Su as she kissed Tusi's cheek.

"Did you like it? Was it good? Where is your sister Sieni?"

"Oh, Sieni is with some other people. She said she will surprise you one day. Oh, people cheered because you were so good Tusi. You know, when you waved to the people, the colour of your small rings was so beautiful. You were so different from the others because of your rings", said Su. She turned her right hand to tightly hold on to the fingers of Tusi's left hand (still wearing the yellow rings), forcing Tusi to walk through the crowd with her.

"Did your friends like our performance?"

"Tusi, everyone loved your performance. Do you know what the girls said to me? They told me that I am a lucky girl to have Tusi as my boyfriend. They all wish they could sleep with you and wear your rings." As they walked, she kept hitting her right thigh with Tusi's fingers which she was holding on to.

"Tusi please, please when are you going to give me one of your rings?" For a long while Su had wanted to be recognised by other students as not just a friend of Tusi's but also his lover.

"One of these days."

"Come on, Tusi, I will give you money and you give me one ring."

"I do not need money."

"So, what do you want Tusi?"

"Nothing special because you give me good food all the time at school."

"Nnnnn, I think I know what you want Tusi. I can tell from your beautiful smile that you want a special thing from me. Well, I don't blame you", replied Su as she held his fingers tightly up against her upper right thigh.

"What do you mean Su?"

"I think you don't like exchanging rings for food, and I think you are right."

"What do you mean?"

"Tusi, you are a brilliant guy and that is why I love you. I think that you want to exchange your ring with my ring", answered Su, hoping that Tusi would say yes immediately.

"I didn't know that you have a ring. Your sister Sieni told me that she also has one. Su, what sort of ring do you have? Is it a metal silver or golden ring?"

"A real natural ring", replied Su in a very low voice biting her teeth as they walked. She held tightly to Tusi's hand and kept begging Tusi to give her one of his rubber rings.

"Su, but how can a daughter of a pastor wear something so unimportant and of such low value as a small rubber ring from a son of an ordinary planter? People of our district will not like that."

"I don't care what people say. To me all things are important including your small rubber rings, Tusi."

"Su, but your ring may be too small or too large for my fingers. My rings are okay because they are rubber and can stretch to fit any finger, large or small, but if yours is made of metal that could be a problem, especially if it is smaller than my smallest finger."

"We can make it fit Tusi, where there is a will there is a way."

"Waoo, Su that is a great offer. I wish I had a metal ring to exchange with yours. I also wish one of my fingers will fit your ring", replied Tusi dreaming that his fingers would fit whatever kind of ring Su had in her possession.

With a tight grip on his fingers and placing their joined palms on her upper thigh, Su spoke, "I can feel that your fingers are more than hard to fit my ring Tusi. Yes, they are, move, yes move, yes move, yes, Tusi that is great. Would you give me one of your rings now?"

"I wish I could but there are so many people walking with us and I do not want my friends see me giving you one now. I will give you one or possibly two, tomorrow", answered Tusi letting his left hand relax under the control of Su.

"No, Tusi come tonight, tonight I beg you Tusi. I will wait for you in my sleeping net when everybody is dead asleep okay? My net is at the seaside of our small house at the back. Only my grandma and I will be sleeping in that house tonight. Will you come?"

"Okay, but if I forget to come then I will give it to you tomorrow."

Fenika, who was walking close by, overheard most of the discussion between Su and Tusi especially where Su invited Tusi to exchange rings in her sleeping net tonight.

"Hi Tusi, how are you feeling now?" asked Fenika.

"Boy, after that long show I am very hungry my friend."

"Come, let's run to our house to check if there is any food left", said Fenika. When they arrived at the house, Fenika said, "Tusi, wait outside while I go inside to check for food."

In the food safe, Fenika discovered fish, corned beef, pork leg, taro and *palusami* (taro leaves with coconut cream). When Fenika opened the safe, Fenika's sister Lei said, "You shouldn't eat all of the food because mum left it aside for tomorrow's staff meeting."

Fenika ran outside and informed Tusi of what Lei had said, adding, "I am very sorry my friend."

"Oh well, bad luck, we will just have to wait until tomorrow. I am really hungry, but I don't have the energy to walk to Fou's house and check for something to eat tonight", answered Tusi thinking about conserving some energy for his rendezvous with Su later.

"Tusi, you are my very best friend and you know that I would do anything for you because you never at anytime refuse anything I ask of you?"

"Fenika, that's what friends are for. I am hungry so what do you want of me?"

"Tusi you are a special friend to me. Tonight, everyone at the concert was in praise of your name. People talked about your distinct style with your special rings on your fingers. Tonight, I want to show the boys that you and I are best friends and as best friends we share the special rings. So, I ask of you to give me one of your rings and I will collect whatever we can eat out of the food in our safe. I promise to give your ring back tomorrow and if you come late to school tomorrow, I will give your ring to Su to pass on to you."

"Fenika, give me your small finger my friend, special things for special friends, the rings of friendship and solidarity. If you lose this ring our friendship is broken", replied Tusi. After receiving the ring, Fenika hurried inside to prepare two big plates of food.

"What are you doing and where did you get that ring? Isn't that Tusi's ring?" interrupted Lei as she watched what Fenika was doing.

"I am taking some food for Tusi who is waiting outside. Tusi gave me this ring to wear, just for tonight, to show the boys that good friends like us share amongst ourselves."

"Brother, go and call Tusi to come inside while I prepare the food for the two of you. That is a rude way of treating your friends. Go, go, go", said Lei while setting the mat of food for the boys.

When the boys came in, Fenika prepared two cups of *koko Samoa* (Samoan cocoa drink) for Tusi and himself. Lei, who was wearing a thin top and an *ie lavalava* (wrap around) because she was ready to go to sleep, rushed over and gave Tusi a big long hug. She wrapped her hands around his neck, rubbed her breasts against Tusi's chest and brushed her left cheek across his mouth as she turned her head to repeatedly kiss Tusi's left ear and whisper, "You were so outstanding tonight Tusi. I was so happy with your performance. Your rings made you so different from all other actors tonight. I love you. I will dream about you tonight as I sleep, Tusi."

While the boys were eating their food, Lei sat cross-legged near Tusi and talked about this and that of the concert. The conversation was nothing else but the success of the concert and the super performance of Tusi. When the topic of conversation moved to Tusi's rings, Lei asked, "So Tusi when are you giving me one of your rings since I am also one of your very good friends?"

Before Tusi answered, Fenika interrupted, "Tusi let's go. I think we are late."

"Shush Fenika, don't be rude. I am asking Tusi not you."

In a quiet voice Tusi replied to Lei, "Thank you very much for the nice food. I feel very energetic again for another show. Sorry Lei for our disturbance keeping you awake at this time of the evening. Nnnnnn, one of these days I will certainly give you one of my rings."

"That is great Tusi. You make me sleep happily. I look forward to your offer", answered Lei.

Fenika and Tusi joined the rest of the boys who were ordered by the concert management staff to camp together in one of the classrooms that had been used for concert preparation. Tusi unrolled his sleeping mat and lay on his back with hands on his forehead. Because of the long day involvement with the concert and a full stomach, in no time he was fast asleep. Fenika on the other hand lay still and pretended to snore. He thought to himself, "Oh yes, I have got the ring I wanted. I have the strength after good food, so I am now ready for the greatest thing that I have been dreaming of Su Su Su Su."

Once he knew that everybody slept, Fenika quietly made his way through the dark of the night to the house of Su who was waiting with great hope that the boy she dreamt of would come as she had asked. After creeping silently through the dark of the night, Fenika reached Su's house and found the sleeping net where he hoped to find Su.

Slowly, he lifted the base of the net up to make enough space to push his hand through. Contacting warm bare skin he gently rubbed his finger with the yellow ring on it over the body of the sleeping person, desperately hoping he had found Su. The sleeping person felt the fingers touching her belly. She slowly directed her right hand towards the invading palm, took hold of the fingers, and explored them until she found the rubber ring she was seeking. The slow and smooth touch from the investigating palm was a good sign to Fenika but he was still not certain whether the investigator was Su or not. Then the investigator tightly squeezed the invading palm, demonstrating to the invader that he had certainly found his target. She then slowly pulled the invading hand to her belly inviting the invader to come in with care.

Concealed by the darkness, Fenika stole inside the net, and slowly slid under the sheet to lie flat facing the awaiting naked female form. He kissed her forehead and then her right cheek and whispered into her right ear, "Give me your finger and let me give you one of my best rings."

Offering her finger in the dark to accept the rubber ring, the naked Su said, "Oh, thank you, Tusi." Fiddling with the invader's fingers she whispered, "Where are your other rings?"

"Don't worry my other rings are at home." After clamping her hands around the invader, Su started to slowly explore his lower back with her hands. But she hesitated when she encountered a lump with a large smooth scar across it. The discovery of the lump and scar prompted the invader, who had been unsuccessful in putting his finger through the ring of his naked partner, to quietly retreat. Grabbing his *ie lavalava*, he crept out from under the sheet and the sleeping net, and fled home through the rain. On arriving home, he removed his *ie lavalava*, hid it underneath the working clothes in a washing bowl and pretended to sleep under a sleeping mat in their house.

When Su woke up, she was wearing a rubber ring, which to Su could belong to nobody else but Tusi. She kept kissing the ring and silently calling out the name of Tusi, her great lover. Su thought to herself, "Oh yes I am now wearing the ring of Tusi the man of my life. What a blessing and poor Tusi, he tried so hard, but he had to go because of the rain. Oh, poor lover – maybe next time when I hold him again." As Su replayed the previous night's invasion in her mind she recalled her discovery of the lump and the scar on the lower back of the invader. "Yes, when I held him tight, my palm cupped the lump, the lump – but wait, Tusi doesn't have any lump or scar on his lower back – what is this? I am sure I didn't ever see a lump on his back when we played volleyball or practiced for the concert. What is going on? I certainly touched the lump with the scar on his lower back just before he left. Wait, the invader may have been a ghost? Yet, I definitely felt the lump and the scar." In her mind, Su ran through images of the lower backs of all Tusi's friends. "Who else would the invader be? If not a ghost, the only friend of Tusi with a lump on his lower back is Fenika but how could it have been Fenika? How did Fenika come into my deal with Tusi? What was going on? Oh no, oh shit, what a shame if it turns out to be Fenika who came to me last night – but how? Nnnnn, Fenika was walking with us when I invited Tusi – yes, I can recall that, and he probably overheard my invitation, oh shit." Su cursed herself a million times. She cursed Fenika more than anybody else. She also cursed Tusi for she was very doubtful of how Fenika could have got a ring from Tusi.

Despite the self-blame and shame, she still could not resist looking at and kissing the rubber ring and whispering no other name but Tusi. Throwing her hands in the air, Su called out to the universe, "Why, how and bugger you, if you were Fenika. I could smash your head with a rock you bastard. You're a weak dog! That's why you did not have the power like Tusi because my ring is for Tusi not for you, you bastard." Nevertheless, Su was somewhat encouraged by the fact that she was wearing Tusi's ring and that the invader (who she had to admit was most likely to have been Fenika) had not managed to put his finger through her ring.

Pretending to be sick, Fenika stayed home from school for the rest of the week. Su on the other hand went to school with a doubtful look yet wearing the ring to show people that Tusi was more than a friend to her. Su prepared extra food to share with Tusi. She aimed to get hold of him very early before the assembly to clarify her uncertainty and doubts. When Tusi came to school, several girls were appraising Su wondering how she had got the ring from the best conductor of the concert.

"Good morning girls", said Tusi lifting his left hand.

As the girls greeted Tusi, Su with her eyes focused on Tusi's fingers, furtively pulled the ring off her own finger and pushed it inside the left cup of her bra. She then pushed her way forward past the girls, grabbed hold of Tusi's left hand and said primly, "Good morning Mr Conductor. Can I talk to you now mister?"

In his normal calm and humble way, Tusi said yes and Su led him to a spot under a coconut tree. "Show me your hands. Where is your other ring?"

"Well, Su as you know Fenika is one of my best friends. Last night I was hungry, and he gave me food. What do you think I should do in return for his kindness especially when he asked me for a ring? He told me that he would return my ring today. He promised that if I came late to school, he would give my ring to you to give me."

Su quietly pulled the ring out of the left cup of her tiny bra, pushed it onto her finger, and through clenched teeth asked Tusi, "Is this your ring?"

With his eyes widening in surprise, Tusi answered, "How did you get that? So Fenika gave you my ring this morning? Where is he? You see Fenika is a good and honest friend. I am glad Fenika kept his promise to give the ring into your good secure hands if I came late to school today."

Tusi had spoken quite believably as if he was innocently unaware of what Fenika had planned and done regarding the ring so Su was undecided as to what to do next. She didn't know whether to tell Tusi what had happened or to keep quiet. Still wearing the ring from the invader, tears welled up in her eyes.

"What is wrong Su? Did I say something hurtful? Are you disappointed because I gave Fenika the ring but not you? I am sorry. Look you can keep that ring because I meant to give you one today as I said last night. I can still give you another one if you want. Oh, by the way, you still have a promise to fulfill – a ring for a ring – remember?"

"Tusi, I feel very sorry and stupid. I know Fenika is your friend, but I hate him. I was not expecting one of my enemies to give me something I love so much from the person I love. I am sorry but I have to return the ring to you", said Su as she slid the ring back on to Tusi's finger.

"So, what about your promise?"

"A promise is a promise but only when you come – I will let you know when I am ready, okay?"

"Okay Su, to show that you keep your promise you get to hold this ring and when you are ready, I will come with a new ring to exchange with yours, deal?"

"Thank you Tusi, deal."

Due to insufficient funds from the concert, only a small number of students were selected to join the teaching staff on the Pacific trip. Tusi was selected over Fou and Fenika. Lei and Sieni were also selected.

Given her strong feelings for Tusi, Su had planned to invite Tusi to exchange rings on the night before Tusi was to go overseas. Su, who kept no secrets from her adopted sister Sieni, told Sieni all her plans, wishes, and hopes for Tusi as the man for her future. She told Sieni that she (Sieni) would be her bride's maid on her special day with Tusi. Because Su was sick and did not go to school for a few days, she asked Sieni to give Tusi a note. Sieni opened the note without Su's knowledge and read:

"Please accept my invitation to spend your last night with me next week, love Su."

Sieni who also had strong feelings for Tusi decided this was her opportunity to get the boy she was longing for. Without delay, Sieni wrote a replacement note, which said:

"I am ready tonight – sleeping net near hanging blind – seaside of the big house, love Su."

Carefully following the instructions on the note, later that night Tusi successfully found the sleeping net. Under the cover of darkness, he lifted the edge of the sleeping net, crept under the net and lay down under the sheet. Kissing the naked body, he found, he offered her his ring and put the ring on her finger. In return, the naked girl with all her noiseless power offered her ring to be an asset of the conductor.

"That was super Tusi. I promise I will hide your ring in a secret place until we surprise each other again okay?" whispered the naked girl.

"Whatever you say Su but keep it secret. I promise I will also hide your ring in a safe place until we meet again after the trip", whispered Tusi as he quietly left.

Waking very early in the morning before anyone else in her family, Sieni hid her ring in a safe place that nobody else, and especially not Su, would find. She promised herself that she would never wear the ring but would find the right time to convince Tusi about their secret affair. As part of her plan, Sieni also decided to tell Su on the night before the school trip that she (Sieni) had misplaced the invitation note that Su had asked her to give Tusi. This would prevent Su from waiting for Tusi unnecessarily.

The school trip started with a sea voyage from Apia to Fiji on the MV Matua and returned via Tonga, Niue and American Samoa on the MV Tofua. During the trip, Tusi could not forget his first-time ring exchange experience with a naked Su. Every time he looked at Sieni during the trip, he recalled his night with Su and her quiet whispered promise about their next meeting on his return from the trip.

On the MV Matua, the staff and students occupied the top of a sizeable deck with a tarpaulin as cover from the rain and hot sun. The students were well disciplined, kind, and friendly to the other passengers and the crew of the ship. Given the good relationships between the school tour and everyone else on board, the school group offered a free, two-hour show that night for the captain, crew and the other passengers.

After the show, Jack a teenage passenger from America, made friends with Tusi. Jack invited Tusi and other students to play table tennis in the games room on the second floor. While the others were talking and playing table tennis, Jack took Tusi and showed him his room. After telling Tusi that he could come and sleep in his room if he wanted to, Jack asked Tusi to help arrange for him to get together with one of the girls from the school tour.

"That is not a problem Jack. Just let me know which girl and I can arrange that for any time you want." In thanking Tusi, Jack gave him ten American dollars.

While enjoying his beer, Jack talked with various girls in the games room while Tusi played table tennis with some of the girls. Some students were sitting around with other passengers admiring the stars, the moon, the waves, and the open ocean. After a while Tusi was tired so he went to Jack and asked for the key to his room.

"Go ahead my friend. I will be here for a while talking to the girls", said Jack.

"Enjoy yourself my friend. Knock on the door when you come", said Tusi.

Observing Tusi leave the games room, Lei pretended to go to the toilet and hurriedly followed him. Unaware he was being followed, Tusi entered the cabin, switched the light off and jumped on the bed. Just before his head touched the pillow, he heard a knock on the door. Thinking it was Jack, Tusi went to the door and turned the handle. Before he had a chance to open it, the door was pushed open and a youthful female figure forced herself in. "Shhhh, it's me, it's me. Keep quiet. Give me the door handle", commanded the intruder.

The intruder locked the door with her right hand and took Tusi's hand in her left. She threw herself on Tusi and sought him with all her strength and power. There was no asking for permission, no investigation, no examination, no customs, or immigration, no application, nor rents to pay, everything was forcefully free as the MV Matua sailed to Fiji. Movements they felt from left to right, down and up as they closed their eyes. It was as if two beasts were fighting to be one.

"You promised me a ring, so where is it?" whispered the intruder. "Remember you ate the mango flesh so where is my seed, you bugger swine, smart sweet."

"No Lei, remember you bullied me – you bugger swine, stingy bee."

Looking at each other in the semi-darkness of the cabin, they discovered that all their past differences had been erased during the love fight they had just engaged in. They recognised that this marked a new beginning between the two of them and they both promised to keep this new development a secret for now.

When Tusi woke, the intruder was gone but her bra was left behind on the bed. Hiding the bra in his *ie lavalava*, Tusi rushed to the games room that was now empty except for his friend Jack who was sleeping on the bench. Tusi dropped the bra onto Jack's chest and went to the toilet. On his way back he heard talking and laughing. An elderly couple and three white female (*papalagi*) tourists were laughing and trying to wake up Jack. More and more people including some students drifted into the games room and started to play table tennis while Tusi tried to help Jack, still with the bra draped over his chest, sit up. Finally, a drunken Jack half opened his eyes, pushed himself up with a bit of help from Tusi, hung the bra across his left shoulder, and leant on Tusi as Tusi guided him back to his room.

"You've done well, my friend", said Jack as he dropped onto his bed and off to sleep.

A few hours before their arrival in Fiji, Tusi went to check on his friend Jack. He knocked on the door and entered to find Jack was still lying on the bed with the bra wrapped around his neck.

"You did well last night, my friend. I saw you clinging on the shoulder of one of the girls from my tour. You did very well Jack", said Tusi.

"Tusi my friend, you see, after we had a great time last night she dressed and left her bra for me as a reminder of her. Wasn't she great? All of this went well because of you, my friend. I thank you for that Tusi", said Jack with a smile.

"In case I don't see you on departure, I wish you well for the rest of your trip. Sorry I have no money to give you but take this small ring – every time you look at the ring, you will remember your friend Tusi", said Tusi as he put the ring on Jack's finger.

"Thank you, my friend", replied Jack, slipping his hand into his pants' pocket. "Hang on Tusi, give me your hand, this is just something for you to buy you an ice cream with."

The boys said goodbye to each other and Tusi ran upstairs. As Tusi climbed the stairs he opened his hand to have a good look at the paper money Jack had given him. To his amazement he found that it was an American one hundred dollars note. Tusi did not use this money during the trip but instead he safely hid it to take home for his parents.

Sailing back to Apia in Western Samoa by the MV Tofua was very different from sailing away from home. The staff and especially the students were like peacocks – shoulders back, heads high, looking sharp and with a mixture of languages. It was a very proud time for the tour, as if they were coming home after a successful mission to the moon.

As the travellers stepped on to dry land, the waiting relatives and friends rushed in to welcome their children, relatives, and friends. Those who could not make their way through the crowd called out, "Hello, cheers and welcome home." The hearty 'welcome home' greetings mingled with the excited and joyful voices of those returning home. Lots of questions were asked but few answers given for everyone was busy kissing, hugging, crying and shaking hands. The awaiting crowd pressed for answers but the travellers had no time to reply and or even pretend to know but instead nodded their heads to indicate that answers to questions and accounts of their travels would follow later.

On greeting the students, Tusi told his comedian friend Manu to appraise the awaiting students with a short report of their trip.

So, when Su asked Manu, "In Tonga, did you see the queen's turtle?"

Speaking loudly so all of those gathered around could hear, Manu replied, "Oh yes. Tusi and I had a good ride around the palace on a very big turtle."

"How big was the turtle?"

Manu pointed to a turtle shaped Volkswagen car parked on the wharf. "You see that four-wheel drive car? That is how big it was."

"How many legs did the turtle have?"

"Fourteen."

"But we were told in school that a turtle has only four legs."

"That is why I pointed to that four-wheel car because the Queen's turtle has four legs."

"But you said fourteen?"

Manu covered himself by saying, "One of the servants to the Queen said that every ten years for the last 100 years they cut off one leg because the turtle could not eat horse meat." (Eating horse meat is new to most Samoans but a delicacy to Tongans. So, Manu joked that any animal, in this case a turtle, that doesn't eat horse meat is punished – in order to bring his 14 legs down to 4.)

Another girl named Moira asked Manu, "So, what sort of people did you see in Fiji?"

"Black and yellow."

"Why and how?"

"Some people turn black because they drink kava all the time while working in the coal mine and other people are yellow because they eat curry all the time as they cut the sugar cane."

During the school tour, Mala, the mother of Lei and Fenika, had gone to deliver a plate of food for Pastor Maka and his wife Fa'apito. Mala remembered the *ie lavalava* she had found in her washing the day after the school concert which she had hidden away in a secret place. Printed clearly on the *ie lavalava* was the name Susana Maka. So, Mala wrapped the *ie lavalava* in a small newspaper and took it along with her to check with the wife of the pastor if the *ie lavalava* belonged to them.

After presenting the food to Fa'apito, who was preparing a cup of *koko Samoa* (Samoan cocoa drink) for her elderly mother Emele, Mala sought permission of Fa'apito to speak to her about something else if Fa'apito had the time. Meanwhile, Mala showed her respect to the wife of the pastor by helping Fa'apito to take the koko and a plate of food to Emele. Mala kissed Emele's cheek and offered the older woman love from her husband and children. Mala picked up a few empty cups lying near Emele, washed them in a bowl of water, helped Fa'apito to organise the plates and cups on the small table near the food safe and asked Fa'apito if there was something else, she could help her with.

"Oh no, Mala, thank you very much for helping. Come sit down. Get that cup and we can have koko Samoa and the nice *faalifu* you brought, as we talk", said Fa'apito.

"You go ahead with your morning tea Fa'apito. I had mine before coming. Thank you very much for your hospitality", replied Mala placing the wrap she had brought near her left leg.

"Oh well, I hope you don't mind me eating something? And what is that you would like to talk about?"

"Please Fa'apito excuse me and forgive me if this is irrelevant or if it causes some trouble to you and your family. On the day after the school concert I found an *ie lavalava*, which does not belong to our family but has the name Susana Maka printed on one of the corners. So, I thought that it was worth bringing it to you to see whether it is one of yours. After talking to my husband and children we really have no knowledge of how it came into our home", explained Mala while opening the parcel containing the *ie lavalava*.

There was silence as Fa'apito inspected the *ie lavalava*. Fa'apito cast her thoughts back to something her mother Emele had said the morning after the school concert. Emele, who had slept in the same house as the girls on the night of the concert, told Fa'apito that she had heard a noise like somebody running out of the house during the night.

Not long afterward, she heard a dog barking in the distance, as if it was chasing something. Given her age, Emele was not sure whether it was a dream or not. Yet on the morning after the school concert when folding the girls' sheets, Fa'apito found an *ie lavalava* which did not belong to her family. Fa'apito hid this ie lavalava in a secret place so that none of her children or her mother would wear it.

"Thank you so much Mala. That certainly is my daughter Susana's *ie lavalava*."

"Oh, that is great. I am glad I brought it. I'm sure Susana would be very happy to get her *ie lavalava* back."

Feeling a bit hot, Fa'apito excused herself from Mala and walked over to her box of clothes. After digging out a small package, she brought it back with her and sat down near Mala again. Fa'apito took some long deep breaths while continuing to smile. As she unwrapped the package, Fa'apito asked Mala, "What about your family, have you lost an *ie lavalava*?"

Mala replied, "Not that I know of. Why?"

"Well, on the morning after the concert, I found an *ie lavalava* in our house (not mentioning that the *ie lavalava* had been found tangled in Su's sheet), so I wrapped it up and put it away", said Fa'apito as she flattened the *ie lavalava* in front of Mala.

"Oh yes Fa'apito, I remember now, I bought an *ie lavalava* of the same colour and size for Fenika. That is right."

"Yes, you are right because the name Fenika. P. (P is for Pito the father of Fenika) is printed at one of the corners with avocado stain."

"Thank you Fa'apito. You saved me from buying another *ie lavalava* for Fenika. Isn't it a coincidence that I have brought you the *ie lavalava* of Susana?"

"Yes it was great for you to do that Mala but unfortunately I won't give you Fenika's *ie lavalava* because after informing the council of chiefs about something else, the council advised us to withhold anything we could find as evidence to that case."

"Would you mind if I asked what that something else is about please?" begged Mala, feeling very scared that her son Fenika may have been involved in that something else.

"I wish I could tell you but the whole matter is now under investigation by the council of chiefs."

"If it's something to do with the *ie lavalava*, then I really believe it was a mix up when the students were dressing and getting back into their uniforms after the concert, wasn't it Fa'apito?"

"I don't know because I also found a rubber ring – you know those rings that were worn by the master conductor, Tusi?"

"Oh yes, did you find a ring too? Well there you are, Tusi was the only kid with those special rings – but as far as the *ie lavalava* are concerned I am sure it was a mix up of uniforms when the kids packed up after the concert."

Feeling guilty and fearing that something may have gone wrong somewhere in the past involving her son and with regards to the exchange of the *ie lavalava*, Mala apologised to the wife of the pastor. When Mala left, she gave a ten tala note ($T10.00) to the wife of the pastor – a culture of respect given to the people of God in Samoa.

After evening prayers on the first night at home from his school tour, Tusi shared the news of the trip with his parents and sisters.

"Did you enjoy the trip son?" asked Mum.

"Yes, Mum, it was a good trip. I saw so many kinds of houses, animals, birds, and people. I also made a lot of friends", replied Tusi as he unwrapped the packet of arrowroot biscuits, he had bought home for the family.

"Thanks for the biscuits. So, what did you get for Mum and Dad besides the biscuits?" asked his sisters.

"This is a surprise Dad", said Tusi. Digging out his sheet from his suitcase, he untied the knot at one of the corners and handed a small, knotted handkerchief to his dad.

Pau turned the knotted handkerchief over and back before opening it and asked, "What is this Tusi?"

"Just open it, Dad. Open it."

Laughing, Pau slowly opened the knotted handkerchief.

"Wao, look at that! It is a one hundred American dollars!" exclaimed the sisters.

"Where did you get this money from Tusi?" asked Pau.

"Well, Dad you know the rings for marking our chickens that I like to wear? I gave one to the boy from America whom I made friends with on the MV Matua and in return he gave me one hundred American dollars (US$100.00)."

Pau and wife shook their heads and because Pau was still in doubt, he asked Tusi again, "Tusi are you telling the truth?"

"Yes, Dad I am telling the truth. Just before the MV Matua arrived in Suva I went to say goodbye to my friend Jack. I gave my friend the ring as a gift to remember me by. In return, he put his hand inside his back trouser pocket, dug out something, and placed it in the palm of my hand as we shook hands and said farewell. Without checking what he gave me, I thanked him and left. I knew it was paper money, but I didn't know the amount until I had a good look later as I was running up the stairs to where we were staying. Because the amount was too much, I decided to keep the money and give it to you to buy more rings for marking our chickens."

"Okay son, I thank you for your decision to give us the money. This is much more than the real value of the chicken rings, but we will make sure we use it wisely", replied Pau.

After the evening meal, Pau and wife questioned Tusi, given the local news about the *ie lavalava* and chicken rings found in the house of the pastor. "While you were away on the Pacific tour, there was news that an *ie lavalava* and a chicken ring were reportedly found in the house of the pastor, the day after the school concert, did you have anything to do with those things Tusi?"

Tusi hesitated as he tried to recall what had happened. "No Dad, remember I was sleeping at school with the boys on the night of the concert?"

"Yes, the teacher confirmed that, but the ring found was yours because you were the only person wearing those rings. What do you have to say about that?" asked Pau.

"Dad, I remember I gave my friend Fenika one of my rings that night. Fenika gave the ring to Su to give to me and I gave the ring back to Su because she wanted one – that is why Su still has one of my rings."

"Son, did you get any money for the ring you gave Su?"

Tusi laughed and replied, "No Dad, how much do you think I should sell the ring to Su for?"

"Son, the rings are for marking our chickens not for selling to the girls." Pau laughed and continued, "Now son, I understand that you enjoy wearing our chicken rings but given the current investigation by the council of chiefs about the complaint of the pastor and his wife, I ask you to stop wearing the rings as from now."

"Okay Dad, I promise I will not wear the rings again."

Immediately after Sieni returned from the trip, Su explained in detail the news about the *ie lavalava* and the chicken ring. Su told Sieni that the council of chiefs was investigating whether an intruder had entered the pastor's house on any night since the school concert; and if the suspect were proven guilty, the whole family of the intruder would be forced to leave the village according to the Samoan culture. Su also told Sieni that her father might be facing dismissal from his position as pastor of the church if his children were proven to be the cause of the problem.

"Who do you think are the suspects?" asked Sieni.

"The only names mentioned so far are Tusi and Fenika because of the chicken ring and the *ie lavalava*."

"Did anybody see them coming to our house at any time on any night after the concert?"

"I don't think so."

"Did you say anything to our parents?"

"I told Mum that Tusi gave me the ring but as for the *ie lavalava* I told her I don't know anything."

"Do you think they will ask me?"

"They were waiting for you to return so they could speak with both of us."

When their parents brought up the issue at home, Sieni explained that after the concert, everybody was rushing around cleaning and packing to go home. During this chaos, Sieni had packed their clothes and dancing uniforms. When they got home Sieni realised that she had mistakenly packed a different *ie lavalava*, of a similar colour to Su's, with Su's uniforms. When Su asked for her *ie lavalava* before going to bed on the night of the concert, Sieni gave her this new *ie lavalava*. Sieni also supported her sister Su by telling their parents that Sieni and other girls had seen Tusi giving the chicken ring to Su at school when they were playing 'which one' guessing came.

The explanation from the girls somewhat convinced Pastor Maka and Fa'apito that the exchange of the *ie lavalavas* was a mix up in packing after the concert and the chicken ring was a matter of teenage games amongst themselves. In the end, Pastor Maka and his wife Fa'apito withdrew their complaint about the chicken rings and the late-night intruders from the council of chiefs.

Chapter Seven

Big decisions about future paths

The news broke that Tusi was one of the students from the district school selected to continue his education at a high school in Pouli on the opposite side of Savai'i Island to where Tusi lived. Tusi's parents received the news with great joy and thanksgiving to God. Tusi's relatives and friends were also very delighted.

But Tusi was undecided about whether to take up this new opportunity. His plan after he had finished at the district school was to persuade his dad to take him to Loga wharf in Savai'i, and look for an engineering job on the small ferries travelling between Savai'i and the island of Upolu (where the town of Apia and Faleolo Airport are located). The main reason for Tusi's plan was to escape studying and plantation work – the very things Tusi disliked most. So, when he received the news, Tusi was in limbo because even though he would be escaping plantation work at home he would still be facing studying again at the high school.

Other factors influencing his decision were his strong relationships with his female friends, namely Su and Lei. Tusi even thought that he could face plantation work at home if that would mean he could maintain his relationships with Su and Lei. Schooling for future life had never been a high priority for Tusi and in going to Pouli, he knew he would be downhearted and homesick because he would miss spending time with the girls he liked.

One day Tusi had a good long discussion with Lei before they joined the District Youth Conference led by the pastors and their wives on 'Preparing youths for the future'.

Lei was a beautiful young lady and very popular amongst the teenagers. Her seductive manner captured the attention of many of the older boys and young men. To secure her relationship with Tusi, Lei encouraged Tusi with the idea that his future would be more secure with the plantation than going away to school. She wanted Tusi to stay and help his parents with the plantation and promised Tusi that one day they would elope and go and stay with her aunty in the town of Apia. She suggested that Tusi could then become a *supokako* (assistant driver) of her aunty's bus and therefore escape studying and plantation work altogether. Lei's plan seems to fit the kind of life Tusi was looking for.

"Lei, I like your way of thinking because it doesn't involve plantation work or studying after all."

"You see darling, I am a very good adviser, so stick to the plan and just let me know when you are ready. Since we became very close friends, my mother and I have discussed the kind of things you and I should do together to live a happy life."

"That is very good of you and your mother, but my concern is my parents because their preference is for me to go to Pouli."

"And what is wrong with you deciding not to continue schooling and not doing plantation work but doing something different that would match up with the kind of life you want?"

"I suppose nothing is wrong with your suggestion but if I decide to follow your plan then it means that I will disobey my parents and obey you instead, which I don't think is a good thing to do."

"Okay, I understand you love your parents, but would you force yourself to do something you don't like doing?"

"Well Lei, I don't think it is a matter of forcing. My parents would prefer me to go to Pouli or otherwise to stay and do plantation work at home. They have given me a choice between the two things. What to do is my choice because I will be the one facing the consequences. Unfortunately, my choice is between two things I dislike. But regardless of how much I dislike these two things, I must decide which one of these to do, to show my obedience to my parents."

"What if after you obey your parents and go to Pouli you don't get the benefits from more study and more knowledge that they are talking about?"

"Well bad luck to me."

"In that case you will blame your parents."

"No Lei, I would never blame my parents. If I didn't gain the knowledge and good results and useful qualifications after all, it may mean that my choice was not the right one or that my choice was right, but I didn't do a good job."

"And you didn't do a good job because you didn't like what you decided to do?"

"You may be right but, in my upbringing, my grandma told me that obedience goes with willingness and honesty. She said that with obedience, you are developing the willingness to do something regardless of how you like or dislike it, and if you do that something with honesty then you will have all the chances of getting the complete result without doubt."

"For example?"

"Okay, for example, if I obey your plan and your advice to stay home because of our sexual relationship then I am developing the willingness to have sex with you to the best of my ability, and if we did that with honesty we will surely be getting as many children as we want, without doubt, isn't that right?" said Tusi laughing.

"I don't know Tusi, don't get on my nerves."

"Okay bully." They both laughed as Tusi continued, "Anyway what if I obey you and we have so many children and I never become a *supokako* anyway because I don't even know whether your aunty has a bus or not?"

Disappointed at his response, Lei hit Tusi on the belly, "I still believe that you have a right to tell your parents that what they want is not what you want for your future."

"Certainly true, I have the right to tell my parents what I want but remember Lei, our parents have many years of knowledge, skills and experience. We are only small coconuts (the nickname for islanders). We voice our wants, then listen and make best use of the advice given. Our future then depends on our choice to obey or disobey. I don't know about you but that is what my grandmother told me when I was an even smaller coconut."

"What did your grandmother tell you?"

"She kept reminding me that kids who listen to and obey their parents will truly be rewarded with something good – we don't know."

"Parents are not always right in their ways and direction to their children."

"I understand that Lei, our parents are not always right. At the same time our parents may tell us something that is right but because we dislike it, we think it is wrong."

"So?"

"That is why I always ask and discuss matters with my parents because they know more than me and I may bring something new to them. In some, if not all, cases my parents change their mind once they understand my views. While they have the right to direct me, they also give consideration to my views and in the , they always give me the choice because I will be facing with the consequences of my decision."

"In other words, even though you dislike both studying and the plantation, you will still choose to do one of them because of your commitment of obedience to your parents?"

"I think that is the case Lei."

"If that is the case then you intend to ignore my plan all together ah?" asked Lei, trying to think of another way to win the mind of Tusi.

"Not really. As I said before, it was a good plan, but I am doubtful about its outcome. At least I can see why my parents are directing me to doing plantation and schoolwork because surely if I work hard in our plantation, I will get food and if I work hard at school, I will gain that new knowledge and understanding. Isn't that right?"

"My dear Tusi, say your parents die tomorrow and you love me as your girlfriend and wife what is your commitment of love?"

Tusi laughed and said, "Well, if that is the case as you stated then I suppose sex is my commitment? I don't know."

"That is not a bad commitment and surely if you stay and help your parents with the plantation you won't miss out on reaping full benefits because I will be with you at all times."

"Knowing you Lei, I think I believe you. You are a beautiful girl with a well-known record amongst the males of our district. However, if I don't go to school in order to satisfy our desire for sex then our future is very risky and shaky because we have no plantation and I am unsure of any *supokako* job from your aunty. You also don't know whether you will be getting any job to feed us and whatever number of children we would have, not to mention other children you would probably get from your other lovers ah? By the way, what is your commitment of love if I obey you and your plan?"

"Well, Tusi, what else do you want if my whole brown body is available at all times for you? And what more do you demand if your obedience to me is rewarded with no more study and plantation work? You will wake up not to drive but to ride a bus everywhere; you will collect the fares and give or keep the change from the passengers; you will make your pay first before giving the rest to my aunty; you will come home from shopping with new clothes and food; and straight to the shower while your lover sets your mat with the food of your choice. In the moonlight I will walk you to see the waves come and go; and have sex anywhere if we can't have it at home – that is my kind of commitment. It is your choice."

As he listened, Tusi followed the movement of Lei's sexy eyes. "Your words are sweet like your left eye and smooth like your right eye; you tackled my feelings and persuaded my mind to your kind of free life. I am delighted and fall in love with your offer Lei but how can I escape my commitment to my parents and seek forgiveness from them?"

"Don't worry Tusi, parents normally forgive their kids after a while. They don't retain hatred forever because they learnt to forgive quickly and after all Jesus has died already to forgive any wrong, we do. Your parents may be disappointed for a few minutes, but all will be well before sunset."

After Lei's seductive talk, Tusi felt more and more drawn to Lei and seemed to bow down to the sex trap Lei had set.

Tusi thought to himself, "Why then would I worry and sweat anymore with school and plantation work if I could get this free service from the lady I tend to love? I will be a chief *supokako* with a beautiful princess at my side at all times, collecting money, paying myself and eating dinner made from the best food of my choice before the moonlight joy every night, how could I refuse that?"

Lei added, "That is only part of your reward and providing you promise me now that you will obey my plan you will be getting plenty more after the conference. Better still, if you promise now, we can even make things start happening much more quickly, even before the conference."

When Tusi and Lei joined the Youth Conference, it was obvious to the crowd that close relationship had developed between the two. Lei followed Tusi everywhere, telling her friends about their close relationship and their plan to get together in the very near future. She told them that they were particularly interested in joining the conference because they wanted some ideas of how to prepare themselves to elope. On the other hand, Tusi who normally hung around with boys in community gatherings seemed to join the female groups more because of Lei. He couldn't separate himself to speak with other people without asking Lei's permission.

After a day of group discussions and training, the conference ended with a service led by Pastor Maka, the father of Su one of the girl friends of Tusi. In the service, Tusi sat together with Lei and most of their friends awaiting the teaching and message through Bible readings and sermon.

Pastor Te'o took the stand for the Bible readings. "Here is our first reading: 'My son, obey your father's command, and don't neglect your mother's teaching. Keep their words always in your heart. Tie them around your neck. Wherever you walk, their counsel can lead you. When you sleep, they will protect you. When you wake up in the morning, they will advise you. For these commands and this teaching are a lamp to light the way ahead of you.' Amen.

Our second reading provides some commands and teachings that will keep you from immoral women, from the smooth tongue of an adulterous woman: 'Don't lust for her beauty. Don't let her coyness seduce you. For a prostitute will bring you to poverty.' Amen."

Afterwards, Tusi, who had been impacted spiritually during the service, tried to depart for home but Lei held him back. She again tried to win the mind of Tusi and to stop him from going away to school.

"I know how you feel because of the service. You can still obey your parents by choosing to stay home and help with plantation work, but it is all up to you. Just remember that I commit myself to you. I may be attracted to other men but never a prostitute."

"Thanks Lei, I think the service reminded us of what to do. We can still be very good friends, but tomorrow is another day. Who knows what will happen tomorrow?"

Su, the other girl friend of Tusi, encouraged him to go to school at Pouli and later join the theological college with a special plan for a big wedding between the two of them after Tusi's graduation. Su wanted Tusi to become a *faife'au* (pastor) and she would be his wife and look after the Sunday school.

"Congratulations Tusi, you deserved to be selected for further study at high school because you are a church loving lad. Your selection was not a surprise to me because I know that you are always doing the unexpected and above all you are naturally blessed with a lot of things because you never missed Sunday school, youth groups and church on Sunday."

"Thanks, Su, for the compliment but I am still not convinced because as you know, I not only hate studying but I will miss you. I wish the option was for me to go and work in Osa's mechanic shop instead of studying in Pouli so that I could still see you during the week."

"But you shouldn't worry because my sister Sieni was also selected and will be going with you to Pouli which means that I can go and visit my sister and of course you, my husband to be, about every fortnight."

"That is not a bad plan, but it doesn't remove the studying."

"Tusi, wherever we go and whatever we do, always involves at least some study. If full-time study really bothers, you then I think I have a good option for you."

"What is that?"

"As I have told you before, a lot of people in our village including my parents think that you would be a very good pastor. Given that you hate the idea of full-time study, I don't think you would join a theological college as I would have liked you to. Instead, my dad, as a qualified pastor, said that he can supervise your biblical lessons at home together with practical work which is basically preaching the Word of God in different villages to get experience and improve your skills before he could recommend you for acceptance in the Lay Ministry Program of the mother church."

"That is a very interesting idea."

"Tusi, of all the jobs in Samoa, the *faife'au* is the top because the *faife'au*, not only is the most respected person in any community but receives the best of everything according to the culture of Samoa."

"Su, I like your way of thinking because I would then do everything in our village and of course be here with you. That is a fantastic idea. Unfortunately, I decided a long time ago that I would not take up *faife'au* as a job."

"Why not?"

"I believe what my Grandma told me. She said that the *faife'au* is a representative of God and only God would select and choose His representative. Don't ask me how because I don't know. My Grandma also told me that the respect of the people and the receiving of the best of everything according to the culture of our country are only bonuses for a pastor."

"Tusi that is why being a *faife'au* is the best job in our country because of the bonuses. Don't you like the bonuses? You have the potential and boy you would have no difficulty in reaping the bonuses!"

"Of course, I like the bonuses. Who wouldn't like receiving the very best food free from village families every day and gifts from cultural events and occasions all the time? But, as explained by my Grandma, being a real *faife'au* is not about bonuses. It's about accepting the call from God to preach the will of God and that is why

God alone is the selector – not you or me or anybody in our village and in the world."

"Tusi you are talking about heavenly things. We are down under, so we do what man does. People strive for jobs with high benefits and bonuses like those given to the pastor. Did you know that even the people with skills in other demanding fields of work, quit those fields and join the ministry because of the enormous benefits? Why are you laughing?"

"Because as you spoke, I remembered a conversation with my Grandma when we were fetching water from one of the springs on the beach one day?"

"What did she talk to you about?"

"She told me that she predicted Samoa would be full of faife'aus of the bonus because churches are becoming more like businesses than places of worship. Given the enormous bonuses, lots and lots of people would self-select themselves as candidates for *faife'au*, families would encourage their children to enter the ministry and selection would be controlled by man not God; theological colleges will be full of students of all ages and the supply of pastors will be so high that nearly every family in Samoa will have one or two or more pastors."

"So, what is wrong with that?"

"I don't know, but she said that if her prediction was correct then there would be lots of disappointing changes in the way people worship

God in different denominations. Unfortunately, she said, these changes would disadvantage everybody including the bonus providers and the ministers (faife'aus) and may cause people to knowingly do all sorts of wrong things. Then the problem, according to my Grandma, is that people think that when they do the wrong thing, they can escape, only to discover later that the wrong thing they did has quietly been breeding serious consequences."

"That is great prediction but remember we are down here on earth not in heaven."

"True but whatever we plan and do down here on earth without approval from heaven, then destruction is always a possibility."

"But who cares, we will all die."

"True but it is better to die knowing that you would go to heaven rather than going to hell."

"So, what then do you want to do instead of going to study in Pouli and or training to be a pastor?"

"I want to work as an engineer because I will earn what I worked for."

"Well, I have an uncle named Pio who is a retired minister living in Uli village about four hours away by bus. My father mentioned that Pio is looking for a youngster who he can train in biblical ministry while assisting with his mechanical work. Tomorrow, my parents and

I will go and visit Pio and I will ask my father to talk to Pio about a job for you, how about that?"

"That is not a bad idea providing my parents will agree."

On his return from visiting Su's uncle, Su's father spoke with Tusi's parents. He informed them about the offer of a mechanic job for Tusi with his brother which could commence as soon as possible. The parents of Tusi thanked Su's father and told him that they would investigate the matter and decide about which school or job or area their son would be attending to in the future.

Conscious that his parents were very excited and proud about him being selected to go to high school, Tusi knew that unfortunately they would never accept any alternative to going to Pouli. His parents were totally focused on him going to Pouli. So, one-night Tusi had a conversation with his parents.

"Dad and Mum, there are a few things that I need your advice about. First, I don't feel like continuing to study at high school. I tend to believe that I can do a lot better in helping you with our plantation than going to school", said Tusi trying to frame an excuse.

"Well son, we are so proud of you. You have done so much better than most of the children of our village. Yes, I know that you can help me with the plantation but not now. At present, I believe the opportunity you have been given to gain knowledge in higher and better schools is your gift from God and I don't want you to miss this opportunity. I believe you need that knowledge in order to give much greater help to your parents, brothers, sisters, relatives, and the extended family in the future."

"The other thing I wanted to ask you, what do you think of the training along with a job as offered by the brother of the pastor? The job seems very interesting to me. I don't know about becoming a minister in the future, only God knows, but the engineering job sounds okay to me."

"Engineering is very good training and a good job, but son, we want you to do that mechanic study in a proper school like those in the town rather than simply learning in someone's home. So, for now, given the opportunity provided, you must go to Pouli."

"Son is there anything else stopping you from going to Pouli besides you wanting to help us with the plantation work?" asked Kika.

"Nnnn, nothing, besides missing my friends."

"Well son, you can make friends anywhere. The opportunity is for you to meet new people and make new friends. You will be so surprised to find that you will probably enjoy spending time with the new friends you will meet in Pouli even more than you do with your current friends. Son, opportunity comes just once. When it comes, make use of it or you will miss it forever", advised Kika.

As the time grew closer to the day of his departure for Pouli, Tusi realised that his parents had worked very hard in preparing what he would take to school. Pau was a very good carpenter and built a cloth box (3 feet by 2.5 feet by 2.5 feet) out of the timbers from their old food *sefe* (cupboard). He included a very small compartment inside the box to keep small things like toothpaste and brush, pens and pencils, torch, comb, coconut oil, a hymnbook and a Bible. Pau made a wooden handle to attach to an old rusted blade to use as a bush knife, which was required by the school.

Kika washed and ironed all the old cloths for Tusi, including two sheets, two pillowcases, and two handkerchiefs which belonged to Pau. With the money they received from selling two baskets of copra at the shop, she bought two school uniforms, two pairs of shorts for sports and as underwear. Kika also cleaned an old pair of thongs for Tusi to wear to school.

Tusi realised that there was no way his parents would support his way of thinking. He could see that his parents had put in a lot of effort to prepare the things he would take to school, making use of their old belongings and rebuilding things from whatever they had – all to make sure he would be well equipped to go to school. In the end, Tusi chose to go to Pouli.

Chapter Eight

The real heartbreaker revealed

It took a night and a whole day to travel by bus from Tusi's village to Pouli. This was not due to the distance alone but because the bus had to stop at Loga wharf, which is the interchange for passengers travelling between the islands of Upolu and Savai'i.

On Saturday before sunset, parents with their children and almost everybody else in the village gathered together at the *malae,* a common gathering place, to farewell the travellers. Many tears were shed, by those who were leaving home for the first time and others who would be gone for a long time, as well as by those staying in the village who knew they would miss their departing friends and family members. Hugs were shared and cheeks kissed. Even some who had previously been enemies cried and hugged each other.

As the bus was loaded with boxes, suitcases, bags of raw taros and root crops, bananas, and people, Tusi went around saying goodbye to his friends especially Fenika, Fou, Su and Lei. The farewell was so emotional that Tusi could hardly say a word. With a hug and kiss, he walked away waving his hand. On the bus, Tusi took a seat next to Sieni, directly behind the driver. Through the window of the bus Tusi shook hands with anybody he could reach.

Su managed to push her way forward and grab Tusi's hand saying, "Good luck with school. I will see you and Sieni next week." Su lifted her left hand showing the rubber ring on one of her fingers while placing a note in Tusi's palm and said, "I will keep this ring until you come back. Love you. I told Sieni to look after you. Love you. Goodbye."

Taking the note and securely pushing it under his belt, Tusi replied, "Thank you Su. Please come next week. Goodbye."

As the bus slowly departed, Tusi blew his last kiss to Lei and Su as people shouted, whistled, and called goodbye. Along with the other passengers, Tusi stuck his head out of the window and called and waved until he could no longer see the people, they had left behind through the leaves of the breadfruit trees lining both sides of the road.

Tusi felt tired as he thought more about his love relationship with Su and Lei. He watched the trees passing by for some time before placing his hands on the back of the driver's seat and going to sleep with his head still turned towards the window. Sieni was also tired and still crying from the emotional goodbyes to her parents and relatives. She leaned forward, placed her left arm on Tusi's right hand and fell asleep. The bus grew quiet and the gentle motion lulled many of the passengers to likewise go to sleep.

After quite some time had passed, and while some of the others were still sleeping, a few of the passengers started to sing. They sang song after song, and favourites were repeated and again. The melodies were so pleasing that people joined in as they woke up. Feeling a warm breath on her face, Sieni opened her eyes and discovered that her face was about an inch from Tusi's who was fast asleep and snoring.

"Hey, Tusi you are snoring like you are playing the background piano for the songs", said Sieni. Pinching Tusi's belly, Sieni tried to wake him. "Tusi wake up. That is enough sleeping. Look, it's almost dawn."

"Oh Su, yes Su, what do you want?" Tusi mumbled.

"Shush Tusi, it's me. It's Sieni not Su. Are you dreaming or pretending to…" Sieni placed her left palm on Tusi's face and tried to pry open his eyes with her fingers?

"Oh yes, Su, what do you want?" Tusi asked as he opened and closed his right eye.

"I want you to wake up because you are talking to Sieni not Su."

"Oh, I'm very sorry Su, where are you?"

"Tusi, I am Sieni not Su", said Sieni as Tusi opened both eyes and finally focused on her face.

"Oh, I'm sorry Sieni. I dreamt that Su found me unconscious in your cooking house. Then Su picked up my naked body and took me to school in a bus that you were driving. Oh, what a dream", Tusi said while recovering from his sound sleep.

"Did you say my sister picked you up naked and took you to school in a bus that I was driving? That is very funny dream Tusi. I think my sister must have done something that really blew up your mind eh?"

"I don't know but Su is a very nice girl. I tend to love her."

"How come you tend to love my sister and yet I was the driver? You should have loved the driver because without the driver you wouldn't have got to school."

"Nnnn, I think you are right, smart girl."

"Tell me. What was it that made you love my sister?"

"Oh Sieni, you know that note you gave me at school? That night, I followed the instructions as directed in the note and that was the night of my life. Su really did something that I can't explain that night. She was the first girl to touch and break my heart and all other things – you know. She made me feel like I was unstoppable and flying around the world forever when we exchanged our rings", Tusi replied as he dug out a small parcel from the bag where he kept his papers and small items.

"Look at this ring. I wrapped it with the note that you gave me from Su."

"Wao, what a beautiful ring!" exclaimed Sieni as she slipped the ring on her left ring finger. She opened the note and read it together with Tusi.

"Do you like the handwriting style of the note Tusi?"

"Oh yes, it is beautiful."

After reading it, Sieni placed the note inside her exercise book and asked Tusi, "Where is the note that Su gave you just before the bus took off last night?"

Tusi pulled out the note from underneath his belt. He opened it and on the note was written: 'Don't worry about anything. I have asked my sister to look after you. Love you Su'.

"Do you like the style of the handwriting of this note Tusi?"

"Nnnn, yes but not as nice as the note you gave me."

Sieni opened her exercise book to a page covered in writing and held the two notes against the page. "Tusi, I want you to compare the style of handwriting in the notes and tell me which of the styles of handwriting in these two notes is the same as my handwriting style in my notebook."

"Why?"

"Because I want to prove something to you."

"Okay, I am definitely sure that the handwriting style in the note you gave me is exactly the same as your handwriting style in your exercise book."

"Are you sure?"

"Yes Sieni, I am hundred per cent sure."

"Okay, let us look at the ring." Sieni removed the ring from her finger. "Did you have a good look at the inside face of the ring when you got it?"

"No why?"

"Look here Tusi. See, there is a tiny carving on the inside face of the ring which says Sieni Apu."

"Who is she?"

"Sieni Apu is my aunty, who I was named after. Before she died, she gave me this ring as a gift."

"Come on Sieni, don't tell me Su stole your ring."

"No Tusi, Su didn't steal my ring but…"

"But what?" Tusi asked showing signs of discomfort.

Uncertain of what Tusi's reaction would be when she revealed the truth, Sieni said, "Promise me that you will not be disappointed if I tell you the truth."

"Sieni, I love the truth. If you lie to me, I will hate you forever."

"And if I tell you the truth you will love me forever, isn't that right?"

"Stop asking questions and just tell me the truth."

"No Tusi, promise me that if I tell you the truth, you will love me forever."

"Sieni, you know that you were the first girl that I looked at, loved, and so on, but I never had the chance to do anything about it. I don't know why."

"Well, this is probably your chance, if you promise."

Tusi really wanted to know the truth now so he replied, "Okay, for now, I promise."

Before Sieni started again she pulled a rubber ring from the right cup of her bra. "Okay, I take your promise and here is the truth. This beautiful rubber ring is yours."

"Yeah! Where did you get it from?"

"Shush and listen or you won't get the truth. On the night you came, you put this rubber ring on my finger. This other ring that you kept belongs to me and I don't have to explain to you because you know how you put your finger through my ring. The ring Su was wearing last night is yours too, but Fenika gave it to her."

"How did that happen? How did you get one of my rings? I didn't give you one. It was Su who invited me, so I gave her a ring."

"My dear Tusi, I invited you, not Su. You have just proven that the handwriting on the invitation I gave you was the same as my handwriting in my exercise book. Look again, see, Su's handwriting on the note she gave you last night is different to mine."

"But the name on the note you gave me was Su not Sieni."

"Okay, Tusi, I did that to surprise you. I wrote the note and I put Su's name on it", admitted Sieni. "Remember, on the night of the concert I told you that one of these days I would give you a surprise."

"Nnnn, that was really a big surprise, more than a surprise. But you sounded like Su when you whispered in my ear."

"Yes, I probably did but the performance that made you fly to the moon that night was the experience of Sieni, the girl you were longing to meet, isn't that right?"

"Sieni wait, I don't believe this. Was it really you who put your ring on my finger? Now I wonder why I was out of the world that night."

"Were you happy about how a driver like Sieni took you for an unstoppable flight around the world that night?"

"You were a real champion girl. A champion of champions. A real instigator, what a surprise! So, when is the next surprise?"

"Whenever you are ready."

"Oh well, oh well. I am glad you told me the truth."

"Why?"

"Because it helps to solve my problem of homesickness."

"Is it your homesickness problem or your chicken ring problem?" Sieni asked laughing.

"Well, which one are you good at solving instigator?"

"Both", Sieni answered pinching Tusi's stomach.

"Tell me something Sieni. I understand that your parents withdrew their complaint. Did they ever find the intruder?"

"Honey, nobody knows the intruder besides me. What would you say if I tell you that Tusi was the intruder?"

"For your information instigator, I was not the intruder. You invited me so I was a guest."

"Tusi you were still an intruder because you came at nighttime while everybody was sleeping."

"Sieni, the truth is, everybody was sleeping except you who was knowingly waiting for your guest."

"So, you are blaming me?"

"I am not but that is the truth about you and me. Without your invitation I would not have come to your house that night."

"Whatever you say, my guest."

"Did Su know that you invited me?"

"Honey, nobody knows about our relationship except you and me."

"Okay honey, what about the *ie lavalava*?"

"The *ie lavalava* belongs to Fenika."

"How did it come to your house? Did you invite Fenika too?"

"Stop being silly honey and listen or I will not tell the truth. I am sure you know that your friend Fenika likes Su."

"No, I didn't know that, all I know is that Su hates Fenika."

"Anyway, Fenika was looking for a way to get Su. According to my sister, Fenika must have overheard her invitation to you on the night of the concert. Then he begged you for a ring so that he could come to Su pretending he was you. After getting the ring from you, Fenika then came to our house and gave the ring to Su. When Su discovered the lump on his lower back, Fenika nervously retreated taking Su's *ie lavalava* by mistake and leaving behind his own *ie lavalava*."

"Oh, now I see. So, Fenika, pretending to be me, went to your house without an invitation?"

"Yes honey. He is the real intruder."

"So, did you tell that to your parents?"

"No, because I wanted to protect my sister and family."

"And protect Fenika and his family too?"

"You could say that."

"So, you buried the truth to save your family and Fenika's family."

"In a way I would say yes. Why are you smiling as you talk?"

"I am just thinking of what my grandma told me one night."

"Tell me, what did she tell you?"

"She said that the consequences of any sin can plague us long after the sin is committed. She used to warn me that when we do something wrong, we may think we can escape, only to discover later that the wrong thing we did has been quietly breeding serious consequences."

"Are you saying you want me to tell my parents, or what?"

"Look, just ignore the whole thing because your parents withdrew their complaint and the case was closed by the council of chiefs. After all, you were the only benefactor given your surprise invitation. You will probably be dead long before any serious consequences catch up with you – so why worry."

"You frightened me honey."

"Why?"

"You are probably alright because what goes around comes around."

"That is true because the world is round but don't worry because the consequences of your actions may not come around until long after your burial. Just prepare for when and if the consequences catch you while you are still alive."

Chapter Nine

The true test of obedience

Tusi was 17 years of age when he started at Pouli High School. At that time, Pouli was the only government high school on the island of Savai'i. Located on the west side of Savai'i and isolated in the bush, about five kilometres from the sea, it was a boarding school for boys and a day school for girls. The girls lived in the villages, scattered along the seaside within about five to twenty kilometres from Pouli.

The boarding school provided its own food through the plantation work of the male students. This was something Tusi did not know until he arrived. The school raised a few beef and dual-purpose cattle, grew root and tuber crops (like taro and taamu), fruit trees (especially lemon), coconut and breadfruit trees. Once every fortnight, the school received a shopping order of few cases of mutton flaps, sausages, porridge and some eggs from Apia (the main town of Samoa, which is located on the island of Upolu about 400 kilometres away by sea).

Like any other boarding school, activities including meals, plantation work, teaching, studying, playing, worshipping, visiting families, rest and sleeping were scheduled at set times during the day and across the week. The hostel was shaped like a five-pointed star, with four open wings (houses) for the boys and one wing with rooms for the warden and assistant warden, all radiating out from a big central hall. In each of the houses, the boys' beds were laid next to each other with boxes of clothes by the windows. The beds were in two rows, allowing a walkway of about one metre through the middle of the house. There were 35 to 40 boys per house. Tusi was assigned to the house called Savai'i.

On Tusi's arrival, the leader of the house who was one of the senior students, welcomed Tusi and showed him where his bed and cloth box would be for the rest of the year. Not long after, a call came for all students to gather in the hall for the welcoming speech by the warden. The warden went through in detail the programs for each day of the week, and the rules and regulations for both on and off the campus. In particular, the warden emphasised the importance of keeping up with the set times and showing good manners both on and off the campus every day. After the evening prayer, the boys were then allowed to go to their houses to prepare for bed.

Before the lights were turned off, the boys introduced themselves to each other and shared whatever food or drink they had brought from home. Those who didn't have any, especially the seniors, went around and demanded food and drink from the newcomers. This demanding attitude was not always welcomed by some of the newcomers and in some cases ended up in fights.

As for Tusi, he shared the food he had brought from home with the two senior boys whose beds were on either side of his. The seniors, who seemed to have sympathy for Tusi, offered their support and protection to Tusi against any bully in school.

When the lights went off there was complete silence for a few minutes. Suddenly, a noise arose. It was a cacophony of boys imitating the cries of different animals and birds. Boys were running in all different directions; windows were opening and shutting; plates and cups were banging etcetera. When Tusi sat up to try and find out what was going on, a pillow banged on his head, once, twice and then followed by a sound as if the person who hit his head ran away. Fighting the pain in his head, Tusi lay down and covered his head with his pillow. While he covered his head, somebody hit his feet, once, twice, and again ran away. When he sat up and reached down to relieve the pain in his feet, another pillow banged on his head. This alternate hitting of head and feet went on for about a minute before his neighbours called out and asked what had happened. Tusi could not answer as he was crying. He could not say a word but dug his fingers into his pillow and clenched his teeth together. Tusi was terrified.

Before the bell rang at 5.30 a.m. for the start of the compound cleaning, one of the seniors, the deputy leader of the house, woke up Tusi.

"Junior, you should have been out of bed a long time ago. Do you have a knife and a sharpening file?"

"I have a knife but no file", replied Tusi.

"Get out of bed while I get a file for you."

Tusi received the file with a word of thanks.

"You better be quick because the starting bell will ring soon", said the deputy and walked away.

Within seconds he returned and said, "Can you sharpen my knife first?"

Without any complaint, Tusi started sharpening the deputy's knife. The senior whose bed was on the left of Tusi's, pushed his knife towards Tusi saying, "Can you sharpen mine too?"

Similarly, the senior, whose bed was on the right of Tusi's, pushed his knife along the floor saying, "And mine too warrior."

When the bell rang, Tusi was still sharpening the deputy's knife. He couldn't sharpen the other knives because the file was rusty and blunt.

"Is that how quickly you handle a simple thing like sharpening a knife?" asked the deputy.

"Boy this file is blunt and rusty", said Tusi.

"What did you say? You came here with nothing and now you complain. That is better than nothing. Listen, from now on you had better wake up earlier to sharpen our knives. If you can't do the job with that file, then use you head. So long as the knives are sharpened your soul will be safe, fullstop."

Because Tusi had complained, the deputy punished him by ordering him to climb one of the coconut trees to collect drinking nuts for the seniors after compound cleaning. Besides Tusi, a few other newcomers, who were being bullied by other seniors for reasons Tusi didn't know, also climbed the coconut trees.

Before plantation work in the afternoon, the deputy called, "Don't forget to sharp the knives." After Tusi started work on the knives, more seniors who had heard of Tusi's complaint in the morning handed Tusi their knives to be sharpened too. When the bell rang for the start of work, there were still a few knives Tusi had not sharpened. The deputy said, "Boy this house needs people who work like thunder and lightning. You are too slow. Remember, the slower you work, the more blunter knives you will be getting to sharp. If you don't finish in time, then you will climb again and again to get nuts for the seniors."

Tusi was terrified but he couldn't do a thing about it. He thought to himself, "Is this what I came here for, to sharpen the knives of these idiots and to climb coconut trees twice a day to retrieve nuts for these idiots? I don't think I can handle this kind of life. Who are they to treat me this way?"

When Tusi was preparing for a shower after work, his neighbour senior asked, "Do you have soap?"

"I think so."

"Look my friend, I left mine at home, can I borrow yours?"

Tusi checked his box and dug out his one and only small bar of sunshine washing soap.

"I only have a small bar of washing soap."

"That is good enough. I'll return it when I finish."

After his shower, the senior gave the bar of soap to the other senior who in turn gave it to another senior etcetera without the knowledge of Tusi who was waiting at his bed. After his shower Tusi's neighbour came back and asked, "Did you get your bar of soap?"

"No, I am still waiting."

"Oh, when I was in the shower somebody called out that he needed the soap. So, I called out to take it because I thought it was you who called."

"I didn't come to the shower, so what shall I do then. I have no other soap."

"Don't worry I will find out who the person was after I put on some clothes."

After dressing, the senior walked casually past Tusi, out of the house, through the hall and stopped to chat with seniors from one of the other houses while Tusi was left sitting on his box of cloths not knowing what to do. Looking at his neighbour idly chatting with other seniors, Tusi said to himself, "What an idiot. He begged for soap and I gave it to him. He cleaned his stinky body, dressed up and is now chatting with other idiots while I am sitting without soap and without a shower. What an idiot! What a liar! What a life this is!"

After his first night and day at boarding school, Tusi was overcome with hate and anger. Besides his anger about the bullying atmosphere, Tusi hated himself for not knowing before leaving his home village that the students were expected to work in the plantation to provide their own food, and that every event was controlled by a set timetable. Given the situation, Tusi was very tempted to quit school.

On his second day, Tusi skipped dinner and quietly sneaked away from the hostel and sat in the dark on the steps of the school building. He went over in his mind every part of the situation in which he had found himself and considered the consequences of going back home. A short time later, Tusi heard somebody coming but it was too dark to know who the person was until a voice asked, "What are you doing here at this time? Aren't you supposed to be with the rest of the boys in the hostel?" The man was a teacher from America. Tusi did not answer and the teacher asked, "Why are you crying?"

"I want to go home."

Still standing behind Tusi, the man asked, "Which island are you from?"

"This island sir."

With a very calm voice the man started to comfort Tusi, saying, "Brother, I am a teacher from America and I also want to go home just like you. If you go home tonight you will be at home tomorrow morning. It would take me four days to get home. Brother, we both came here for a better future for our families and if we want to achieve that then we must try and enjoy this place because we are only here for just three years. If you decide to stay, I offer my help with your schoolwork at any time."

Quietly the man disappeared. The challenge and encouragement from the teacher somehow activated positive thinking in Tusi. He said to himself, "This man said that I came here for a better future – what better future? Well, I know my parents wanted me to come to this school to gain knowledge that I can't get at home for the future of my family. How can I stay, given this bullying atmosphere? To achieve what I came here for, I must enjoy this place according to this teacher from America. How, how, how can I enjoy it with the bullying, working on the plantation all the time and when everything is time, time, time? I don't know. This could be the kind of difficulty Grandma was talking about. She continuously counselled that to face and overcome any difficulty I needed to have the liver, or I will eat chicken shit for the rest of my life. Poor Grandma, I love you."

Tusi recalled the kind and wise counsel of his grandma; the joy, and happiness of his parents on receiving the news of his selection for Pouli; the struggle his parents went through to provide all the requirements for his school regardless of their poor financial situation;

the loving words spoken by his grandma and parents on his departure; and his love for them in return.

Then Tusi recalled the mocking he and his family had faced at home. He realised that if he were to go home, the mockers in his village would laugh again and the mocking would increase and be sustained for the rest of his life; and his parents and family would be sad and feel shame. Above all, by returning home he would disrespect the love and commitment of obedience he always promised his parents. Tusi wondered whether he had the liver, as grandma challenged him, for security and survival.

After a few minutes sitting in the dark, Tusi changed his mind. In that short time, he had built in himself the courage to face whatever was to come. Tusi then prayed to God for help before he rejoined the rest of the boys in the hostel.

After setting his mind to stay at school Tusi went to bed. As he slept, he had a dream: Ete, the chief of all the bullies, gave Tusi an empty coconut shell for his drinking water. Tusi had to fill this shell with water from the stream using his mouth, through a half-centimetre, open eye of the shell. His daily water supply depended on how much water he could put through the eye in five minutes. Every time he took his last drink at night, his mouth was filled with all the food he had eaten during the day. Tusi would then wrap up this backwash food and send it to his parents.

On waking the next morning, Tusi was rather unsettled and frustrated and wondered what the dream was all about. He managed to pull himself together and get moving for the day but later the dream was still on his mind, so he shared it with some of the other students.

"Tusi, I overheard you mentioning the name of this bully Ete, what did he do?" Mosa, another new student asked.

"I dreamt that he forced me to store my daily drinking water in the coconut shell."

"Well I don't know the meaning of your dream but I think your dream was telling you that you need to be very careful and therefore you should try and keep away from that fellow because I heard that he is like a prime minister with the way he controls the senior students."

"What do you mean?"

"I mean that most of the seniors obey his orders and he have the power to tell people to do things in the way he wants, like or dislike it."

"What would he do if you disobeyed him?"

"I don't know but he can do anything."

Vai, another newcomer, joined the conversation, "Look fellows, I heard about Ete. He is no different to us. If he asked me to do something, I will never obey him. I will fight him if he bullies me. I also have cousins in the senior years to help me."

Tusi asked, "So, after fighting what would you get?"

"I don't know but I believe the only way to stop bullying from these seniors is to retaliate, isn't that right Mosa?"

"I don't know but there is always a cost to retaliation that somebody has to pay."

"What do you mean Mosa?" asked Vai.

"I mean you may win or lose, depending on how strong you and your supporters are, but the principal may still expel you from school because fighting is not allowed."

Tusi also related his dream to Sieni, who shared it with her friends Lote and Aiga.

"Sieni told us about your dream, Tusi. She said that you are very disturbed, is that right Tusi?" asked Aiga.

"In a way I am disturbed."

"Why?"

"Because I hate bullying."

"Look, Ete didn't do anything. It is only a dream. However, if he asks you to do something with a bullying attitude then just don't do it – it is as simple as that. If you don't like what he asks you to do, then tell a teacher and don't bother to obey him because once you obey, he will then keep telling you to do whatever he wants. I know Ete because we come from the same village. Ete is a good fellow and has commanding attitude. He is also lazy and loves telling people to do things for him. Most of the time he would do nothing if you didn't obey his demands", advised Aiga.

"What do you think Lote?" Tusi asked.

"Remember, we are just talking about a dream not a true event. But if your dream did come true, would you obey Ete and live with just that amount of water every day? If you think no, then don't obey him. If he beats you for disobeying him then the teachers, if not God, would punish him. I think bullying is a way of life, which happens everywhere you go. Instead of retaliation, I try very hard to ignore it and live my life how I want to. Because I am not a good fighter, I normally run away to avoid a fight", said Lote.

"Whatever you do to others, you will get it back somehow, somewhere. If your attitude is bullying you will be unhappy because you will have no friends", added Aiga.

The boys could visit their families in nearby villages on Sundays, so Tusi went to visit his uncle Aso and aunt Avea. They lived on their small farm next to the main entrance of the school. Aso, a retired teacher, was one of the well-respected chiefs in the villages of the whole district. Aso liaised with the churches and schools and local development groups on matters concerning the well-being of villagers and peace keeping within communities. People looked up to Aso as a counsellor and adviser. During his visit, Tusi had a very educational conversation with his uncle and aunt.

"So, how did you find your first week at school, Tusi?" asked Avea.

"It was okay besides a few bullying incidences from some of the seniors. In fact, after the first night I was very depressed and seriously considered going home", replied Tusi.

"Well bullying is unacceptable, but it has become a common behaviour in schools. In the past, a few new students gave up and went home. I hope you won't do the same", said Avea.

"You know uncle and aunty, after some serious thinking, I made a final decision to stay regardless of the bullying atmosphere in school. After making this decision I went to sleep, and I was challenged with a dream."

"What was your dream?" Avea asked.

"I dreamt that Ete, the chief of all the bullies, gave me an empty coconut shell for my drinking water. I had to fill this shell with water from the stream using my mouth, through a half-centimetre, open eye of the shell. My daily water supply depended on how much water I put through the eye in five minutes. Every time I took my last drink at night, my mouth was filled with all the food I had eaten during the day. I then wrapped up this backwash food and sent it to my parents", Tusi said.

"That is a very interesting dream, what do you think Aso?" Avea asked.

"Well, nobody knows the true meaning of dreams, I can only give my interpretation. In the first place, it seems that this bullying has caused you stress Tusi and that stress will become serious and problematic depending on how you face and respond to the situation. I am sure the principal and staff are still trying to resolve bullying which is an unnecessary and unwanted behaviour especially in boarding schools.

There is a second possible interpretation of your dream – one that you may find very hard to accept but something that could be very useful for your future. It relates to your study and why you are here – I think you must work hard in studying every day. Honest continuous studying is a very hard thing to do, like collecting water with your mouth and filling your coconut shell in five minutes. However, as water is so vital to the body, honest continuous studying is vital to the brain to achieve success in schooling. According to your dream, your drinking water for the day depends on the amount of water you put in the shell. That is, the amount of knowledge your mind gets depends on the amount of honest studying you give your brain, within the limited time available to study.

The important part of your dream to me is the backwash. All the food you give your brain each day will come back to you and that is what you give your parents. That is, if you are dishonest with your study your backwash will be dishonesty and emptiness, but if you are honest with your study, you will reap better rewards and fullness in happiness. These are the kind of rewards you will give to your parents and relatives."

"Thank you, uncle, I felt comforted and thrilled as you spoke", said Tusi.

"Yes Tusi, you see I don't believe Ete or any of the other bullies will go to that extreme and treat you in such a barbaric way. Remember, it was only a dream not a real happening. So, if I were you, I would do something useful and turn that dream into something very fruitful for you and your parents and your relatives, including us", advised Aso.

The advice and counselling from Aso and Avea lodged in Tusi's mind the idea that the only way to success is to have the ake, according to his grandma, to honestly study hard at every possible moment given the limited time available. He felt in his heart the courage to accept bullying as an irrelevant part of his schooling life while setting a goal to focus on honest study of whatever subjects were offered to him at any time.

As time passed, Tusi became more and more of a friend to most of the seniors because he obeyed and just followed whatever was required of him. Surprisingly, even the lazy bully Ete ended up being more of a help than a hindrance to Tusi. For instance, when all the boys went cutting the grass early in the morning, Ete would ask Tusi to stay in the house and complete Ete's assignments so that at prep time at night Ete could copy the completed assignments. Similarly, during the plantation work in the afternoon, Ete would send Tusi to sit under a shady tree to complete assignments for Ete and his friends to copy at night. Tusi believed that God used these lazy bullies to give him the opportunities to study and complete all his assignments thus feeding his brain and therefore placing him ahead of the rest of the class in all of his subjects.

Tusi became good friends with some of the senior female students, especially Sieni's friends Lote and Aiga. Lote and Aiga were one year ahead of Tusi and Sieni. At times when most students were enjoying sports and passing the time with other non-academic activities, Tusi and his girl friends would discuss and debate some educational issue or complete their assignments in the library, a classroom or under a shady tree.

Two afternoons a week Tusi was required to deliver and collect the school's mail to and from the only post office in the district located in the village of Faga, about 15 kilometres from school. Tusi would call upon Lote and Aiga to walk with him after school as he fulfilled his mail boy duties. On their way the three would take time out to rest under trees and complete their school assignments.

At times, the warden assigned Tusi as houseboy for the family of Pati, the science teacher, and an uncle of Tusi's lame female friend Toi. Again, through these opportunities, Tusi was able to get some free time to do more study, to complete his assignments with Toi and to ask Pati about subject matters he could not understand.

In his third year of study, Tusi was one of the students selected by the staff to undertake entrance exams for further studies in higher colleges in the town of Apia. Tusi was nominated for the entrance exam for SPRCTA (South Pacific Regional College of Tropical Agriculture). But Tusi declined the opportunity because unfortunately he had no money to pay his fare and associated expenses.

After a couple of meetings with the principal, the principal told Tusi that he and his wife would like Tusi to sit the entrance exam for SPRCTA and that they would pay all the expenses. This offer from the principal was beyond anything that Tusi could ever imagine. He felt embarrassed and quite speechless, but the principal kept encouraging Tusi to get prepared to sit the entrance exam.

Tusi sent a letter to inform his parents about the offer from the principal. On receiving the letter, Pau and Kika were so happy that their son had been given the opportunity to try for further studies. Although Tusi's parents appreciated the principal's offer, they would not take up the offer because they didn't want the people of the village to spread tales that they could not afford to educate their son. With a massive effort on their part, they managed to get the required amount to meet the expenses for Tusi to sit the exam. Pau took the money to the school and thanked the principal and his wife for their generous offer to Tusi.

To further help Tusi with his expenses, his kind friends Fuifui Uati and Ken Lameta offered free accommodations at their family at Vaimoso village in Upolu because they too would go for the same entrance exam.

Tusi gave thanks to The Lord for the entrance exam was a success and Tusi, Fuifui and Ken were amongst those chosen for further studies at STRCTA.

His friend Sieni was one of the first to congratulate Tusi. "What an effort! Beautiful Tusi. See, you almost missed the opportunity", said Sieni.

"Thank God that I got through the exams, but I don't think I will take up the offer to study at SPRCTA", Tusi said.

"Why not?"

"Well, you know my problem already. The cost of attending the new school is very high and I don't think my family could afford it."

"What a waste of an opportunity. So, what are you going to do when you finish high school?"

"Ete confirmed to me last week that his uncle wants me to start working as a trainee mechanic in his mechanic shop on Loga wharf immediately after school finishes. Ete also told me that I can work with him as an assistant mechanic on one of the ferries taking passengers between the islands of Savai'i and Upolu, captained by his father."

"That is okay, but it would be great if you could go to SPRCTA", said Sieni.

Before returning home after completing his studies at Pouli, Tusi spent his last night at the home of Aso and Avea.

"So, what are you going to do next?" Avea asked.

"The uncle of Ete wants me to start working in his mechanic shop at the wharf as early as next week. So, I'll see what my parents say when I get home."

"Is that the right thing to do after all the good reports we have heard and know about your progress? What about your new school next year?"

"I don't know but..." replied Tusi.

"Yes Tusi, I spoke with the staff especially the principal and his wife and they were quite sad when they heard your decision. They would be very disappointed if you don't go to SPRCTA." Aso spoke with some authority and Tusi listened with respect. "The staff, the principal and his wife and us, your family, understand the reason why you would decide to take up the mechanic position immediately – to get money quickly to help your family. That is good thinking but the amount of money you would get from that job next week will not buy a tin of fish and that will not help the family."

Aso continued, "Son, think of how happy your parents were when you wrote to them about the entrance exam. They ignored everything else in order to work to get the money to make sure your expenses for the entrance exam were met. Your father came to Pouli himself to pay the expenses. Then you did very well in the exam. Now think about your dream and your progress so far – you have put all your energy into studying hard for three years to achieve a better outcome, including being selected for SPRCTA, the best backwash you give us – and after all that you decide to take up a mechanic traineeship which can't buy us a tin of fish? What kind of weak decision is that? You have done so well, now you must keep going further. Your selection to study at SPRACTA is just the beginning of your journey to getting better jobs that would give you even more money to buy *pisupo* instead of *eleni* for our family – so think again and reconsider your next step for next year."

As Aso spoke, Tusi recalled every single pathway he had travelled to get to the point he was now at. "With all my due respect uncle, I thank you for your advice. I think I can handle further studies but the only reason I have doubts is due to the finance required. However, I will speak with my parents and see what they say. I am sure they will support your advice", Tusi said. Tusi thanked Aso and Avea and their family for their support throughout his studies at Pouli and promised them that he would come back someday to visit and help. Likewise, Aso and the family offered their further support should Tusi run into any difficulties in the future.

There was joy and thanksgiving to God in the family when Tusi came home with the news that he had been selected to attend a higher school the following year. The extended family congratulated Tusi and his parents and shared in their pride because Tusi's success also meant the success of the whole family.

While still in the mood of celebration, Tusi caught up with one of his village girlfriends, Lei.

"Congratulations handsome friend, you did well", said Lei as she hugged Tusi and kissed him on the lips.

"Thanks Lei."

"So, you obeyed your parents and now you have got the knowledge that you and they wanted. What then is your next move?"

"Well, my parents, supported by my extended family, want me to continue with further studies."

"More study! Again! But do you still want to do that?"

"Oh yes, I am looking forward to it."

"But that new school is very expensive. Do you think your family can afford the cost?"

"I don't know, but we are trying very hard and we hope for the best."

"I wish you luck, my friend, because as you know our life in Samoa is such that nearly every day there is a financial demand for some stupid cultural event or an unnecessary financial demand from religious denominations and hardly a penny left over for the education of children, not to mention the developing and feeding of immediate families."

"That is exactly why I am worried because we can't avoid the culture and religion. Last week as you know, the council of chiefs fined a cousin of mine eight roasted pigs, two hundred taros and ten cases of tinned fish, for beating the district doctor's son. My parents had to provide one roasted pig and three cases of tinned fish towards the fine (according to the culture of Samoa, if a person is fined, the extended family helps to pay the fine). Now my parents are struggling to get together their financial share for the celebration of the Women's Committee House next week, and their share for the *matai* (chief) title ceremony the following week and so on. As it stands now, I don't think my parents can afford my fees."

"So, what will happen if at the end of your family search you can't pay your fees?"

"I don't know but I may either look for a job or stay home and help my parents with the plantation."

"In other words, you will be back to square one, after wasting money for three years to get that knowledge."

"Well, I may be back to square one but this time I have additional knowledge which surely would help to provide a much better job than the *supokako*."

"Like what better job?"

"I have been offered a job as a trainee mechanic in one of the mechanic shops on the wharf starting as soon as I want but I have to talk to my parents first."

"That is good Tusi. Is that the mechanic shop on the wharf next to Morris shop where I work?"

"Yes, that is the shop."

"If you take up that traineeship where would you stay because you can't travel from our village to work on the wharf every day unless you have a lot of money?"

"I don't know."

"Look, I can help you out if you like."

"How?"

"I am staying with my aunty in her house about ten minutes' walk from the wharf. Nobody is occupying the other small *fale* (house) in the backyard. I am sure my aunty would love to have you stay there."

"That is a very good suggestion, but I don't know whether my parents will agree or if your parents and aunty would allow me to..."

"I can make it happen if you want and don't worry about my parents because they really like you – as you know. As for my aunty, she would be so thrilled because she always talks about you every time, we discuss marriage. Who knows, this could be the beginning of the family we have been planning for so long."

"You mean the family you have been planning?"

"Honey, I may not have the knowledge you have but I have a job which I think would be of great help in getting the money for your further study – how is that?"

"So?"

"So, go and speak with your parents and tell them that you are going to take up the engineering job and then we can both work towards saving for your fees."

Again, Tusi seemed to like Lei's plan so he appealed to his parents.

"No son, helping out on the farm is more beneficial than that short-term engineering job. We will get the money and you will learn more skills from the plantation in preparation for that agricultural school next year", replied Pau.

"But Dad, we need to be sure of the money so that I can be sure of starting next semester."

"Son, don't worry, God will provide."

"What if I defer my schooling next year until we get sufficient funds?"

"No son, you can't do that. A year delay is too long. I am sure we can find a way to meet your fees."

"How Dad?"

"Son, I spoke with one of the teachers of the district school and he told me that some of the students he knew of from that college paid only part of their fees at the beginning of school and then paid the rest during the semester. How would you like to do that?"

"I can try if that can be done."

To encourage Tusi not to give up hope because of their financial difficulties, Pau explained to Tusi that administrators of schools didn't expect all students to pay full fees in the beginning of the semester. He said this was because they understood that farming is the major source of income for their students and it takes a while to plant, harvest and market farm produce.

After a discussion with Grandma, Tusi told his parents that he would go and live with Grandma in the plantation until school started the next year. Then he would avoid wasting time walking to and from the plantation every day and be able to spend more time assisting in planting, harvesting and maintenance on the farm. Besides setting traps for the wild pigs, Grandma assigned Tusi to spend at least two hours a day picking up cocoa seeds from amongst the weeds under the cocoa trees. Hungry rats loved to chew through the cocoa pods and suck the sweet testa of the seeds, and at the same time many good seeds would also drop onto the ground from the damaged pods. According to his Grandma, every single seed was worth something and by ignoring the seeds hidden in the weeds there would be an unnecessary deficit in his school fees. This kept Tusi working hard searching through the weeds for seeds, wherever there were rat-eaten pods on the cocoa trees.

After their prayer and meal one night, Grandma said, "I am very happy with your schooling so far son. I am also glad to see that you willingly help with our plantation activities. But I can see that you are unsettled. What is on your mind?"

"I don't know whether it is worry or what, but I wish we had the money. Do you think we can afford my fees?"

"Son, we will, so long as we keep trying. Keep collecting the dropped cocoa seeds and we will get there", Grandma replied and then she started to sing. Grandma loved singing to herself while discussing issues with people. Sometimes, her singing was loud enough for others to join in, so they would take short breaks from their conversation.

"Grandma, why do you always sing this song when we discuss our family difficulties?"

"Son, when we don't get what we require from our given plantation in time, then we are in the dark, like a lost sailor on a dark night on the ocean. When you are in the dark, don't give up but keep trying because daylight is always after darkness. Provided we do all what we can to the best of our ability we can leave the rest to God because he is the light and the lifeboat. Okay, sing the first verse with me."

1. Light in the darkness, sailor, day is at hand!
See o'er the foaming billows fair Haven's land.
Drear was the voyage, sailor, now almost o'er;
Safe within the lifeboat, sailor, pull for the shore.

"I hope the lifeboat will bring sufficient funds to pay my fees because I don't think I can stand the mocking from the people of our village otherwise."

"Son, the only key to getting the great help from the lifeboat is trust. Always stop winching and worrying but try to do all you can to the best of your ability in collecting the seeds left behind by the rats, regardless of the hardship. Keep pulling for the shore, and trust God will do the rest for anything you can't handle. If you don't have faith in God, all will fail. Come on sing the second verse."

2. Trust in the lifeboat, sailor; all else will fail.
Stronger the surges dash and fiercer the gale,
Heed not the stormy winds, though loudly they roar;
Watch the 'bright and morning star' and pull for the shore.

"Grandma, it is very frustrating to see so many commitments that need to be met with the very low income we get from the farm."

"Son, you are correct, our wants are always a hundred times more than what we get from our small plantation. We can never get enough money to cover everything we want at all times, but we can't allow this opportunity for your schooling to pass. As your father said it can take a little while to get the money from the farm and we are confident that we will get the money for your school fees. Son, keep hanging in there, keep pulling for the shore, and don't give up or you will miss the great help of God. Come on, sing with me."

Chorus:
Pull for the shore, sailor, pull for the shore!
Heed not the rolling waves, but bend to the oar;
Safe in the lifeboat, sailor, cling to self no more!
Leave the poor old stranded wreck and pull for the shore!

"Grandma, do you remember that girl Lei who always mocked me when we were young?"

"Yes, what about her?"

"I had a conversation with Lei, and she said she can help out with my fees."

"Why and how?"

"I don't really know why but I think she likes me. She said that she would help me pay my fees because she works as cashier in Morris shop on the wharf. She even invited me to stay with her family near the wharf, during the week if you allow me to work with my engineering job."

"She can do whatever she wants but your education is our family's responsibility. You must be very careful son with offers of help especially from people who haven't treated you well in the past. Try and think of and learn from your past relationship with Lei and friends. Some help, like what Lei is offering you now, can become a bait, and when you are caught in their trap you could end up worse off than after the bee stings from the mango trap."

"But we need the money."

"Son, you are now hungry for money for your fees and Lei is trying to use that to trap you again because she wants you as a husband. Her offer of money is a bait to attract you to that engineering job so that you can stay with her in her family and do whatever she wants."

Tusi stayed silent but he clearly wasn't completely convinced. After all, Lei's offer was very tempting.

"Do you remember what you said when you were young about getting caught in a trap?"

"I think so."

"Just in case you had forgotten, you clearly said that you did not want to be a hungry pig caught in a trap or a hungry flying fox caught in the spines of the anoso plant. If she catches you, Lei will not release you like we did with the hunting dog. She will feed you with the leftovers so that you can do the hunting while she enjoys sleeping and or talalalala with others and so on."

"Oh, I see. I wasn't thinking that way Grandma."

"Son think wisely and be careful. You are in a different age and time. Don't worry. We will get the money. Leave the poor old stranded wreck and pull for the shore. Come on, sing with me,"

3. Bright gleams the morning, sailor, uplift the eye;
Clouds and darkness disappearing, glory is nigh!
Safe is the lifeboat, sailor, sing evermore,
"Glory, glory, hallelujah!" Pull for the shore.

By the time the first semester began at SPRCTA, Tusi's parents and family managed to get some money to finance only half of Tusi's fees and to pay for his travelling expenses to school. (From his village Tusi needed to travel by bus to Loga wharf in Savai'i, then by ferry to Fanua wharf in Upolu Island, by bus to the town of Apia, and another bus to the SPRCTA compound). Instead of buying any new clothes, Kika made sure Tusi's old clothes were washed and ironed. Instead of buying a new clothes box, Pau used their large old suitcase to take his son's belongings to college.

As the name suggests, the South Pacific Regional College of Tropical Agriculture (SPRCTA) was a college to educate and train students from various South Pacific island countries, including Fiji,

Tonga, Vanuatu, Tuvalu, Cook Islands, Niue, American Samoa, Kiribati and Solomon Islands, in tropical agriculture. After three years of successful study students would then be rewarded with Diplomas in Tropical Agriculture.

Located about four kilometres inland from the town of Apia on the coastal front, the college was about three years old when Tusi registered. The new architectural style of its buildings and the landscaping of its playgrounds in the valley separating the chicken and pig experimental acreage from the school buildings and hostels was one of the attractions for both locals and tourists.

After his arrival at SPRCTA, Tusi went through the administration process and was very pleased when the administration officer gave him the opportunity to pay the rest of his fees by Easter time. After registration, the officer told Tusi to go and choose a room of his choice in one of the student hostels. To have a room of his choice and a room to himself was such a privilege to Tusi. At home he lived in open houses with his parents and everyone else in the family and while in Pouli he had resided with about thirty-five other students in an open house and was not given any choice about where he would sleep.

On his short walk (about 50 metres) to the hostel, Tusi met Tana, who had attended District school with Tusi.

"Is that you Tana? How are you?"

"I am good. What about you? I haven't seen you in years."

"I am very well, thank you. I haven't seen you too for a long while. Where were you?"

"I was at Samoa College."

"What brought you here?"

"I am one of the newcomers and have just finished organising my room."

"Oh, that is great. Congratulations Tana. I have just finished registration and I'm going to look for a room."

"Oh, congratulations to you too, Tusi. There is an empty room between mine and No'o, a student from Rarotonga. Would you like to take up that?"

"I don't mind Tana, sounds good to me."

All the rooms were of the same size. Each room contained a bed, a cloth cupboard and a study table. The partitions between the rooms were about eight feet high and the entrances were just curtaining for privacy from the walkway. With great appreciation Tusi, with the help of Tana, organised his belongings in his cupboard and fixed his bed.

During the first few weeks on campus, Tusi was very impressed and enjoyed the college atmosphere. The services within and around the college were of high standard and very convenient. Students were freer to leave the campus at any time and importantly Tusi hadn't come across any bullish attitudes like those he had experienced in his previous school.

Given the less restricted atmosphere at college, Tusi learnt that some SPRCTA students who had come from high schools in Apia and overseas sometimes didn't attend lectures and practical works. Some students liked going to cinemas in the town of Apia after classes nearly every day, and some smoked and drank beer at times during the week if not every day. These observations caused Tusi to think that most students were bright, of higher standards, and were from rich families.

Tusi made friends with any student he met, whether local or from overseas, a senior or a newcomer. Through Tana, Tusi made friends with Alo, a student from American Samoa who had a lot of money. One night, when Tusi and Tana were studying behind the library, Alo came looking for something in which to boil his half a dozen eggs because he had missed dinner and the dining hall was closed. Tusi thought that this would be a good opportunity to help and therefore make friends with this rich student.

"I can help if you like", said Tusi.

"How?" asked Tana.

"If you like you can wait here with Alo and I will take the eggs to boil. I should be back within the next five minutes."

"We don't mind", said Tana and Alo.

Tusi remembered he had seen an electric kettle on No'o's study table. So, he went and borrowed the kettle, put the eggs inside and filled the kettle with water. He picked up coffee and sugar from his room and went back to Tana and Alo, behind the library.

"That was very quick!" said Alo.

"We are going to have coffee and wait for the eggs to cook", Tusi said as he poured coffee and sugar into the kettle so that Tana and Alo could see, and then plugged the kettle into the wall plug before talking with the boys.

After about six minutes, Alo asked, "When are you going to get the eggs? I'm hungry."

"The eggs should be ready by now. Do you want coffee and eggs or just eggs?" asked Tusi.

Knowing Tusi from district school, Tana suspected something strange was going on. Tana looked up and down and then asked, "Tusi what have you done? Where are the eggs?"

"Tana, sometimes you have to kill two birds with one stone. I cooked the eggs in our boiling coffee. I am sure Alo would like to have coffee and eggs because he is hungry. Otherwise I will pour off the coffee and give Alo just the cooked eggs."

Tana and Alo laughed shaking heads.

"I don't mind having coffee", said Tana.

"Me too", said Alo.

As the boys were enjoying their eggs and coffee, Alo asked, "Whose kettle is that Tusi?"

"I borrowed it from No'o."

Alo laughed and shook his head as he said, "You are a great and strange fellow Tusi."

"What do you mean?"

"When I looked at the kettle and saw those letters A.O., I suspected that kettle was mine. No'o borrowed my kettle two nights ago to boil water for his coffee. My mother bought me that kettle just to boil water not to cook eggs as you did tonight. Well done. I hope what you did, didn't damage my kettle."

Tusi replied, "I think your kettle is a multifunctional piece of equipment especially when you are hungry. Your kettle saved you from hunger so you should thank your mother for buying you the kettle." The boys laughed.

Since the cooking of eggs in the kettle of coffee, Alo became a very good friend and joined the study group of Tana and Tusi. Not very long into the development of their friendship, Alo and Tana learnt about Tusi's financial difficulties. While they couldn't do anything about it, Tana and Alo always helped in paying Tusi's fare to go with them to town for shopping and to go to the cinemas.

When Easter break came, all the local students went home and only the overseas students could stay on campus. At that time Tusi had no money to pay his fare to return home for Easter. Although he considered borrowing some money from his friends, Tusi was reluctant to do so because he didn't want to add to the financial load his parents were already bearing with his school fees. Therefore, Tusi sent a letter to his parents saying that he would stay in college over Easter and asked if they could send whatever amount of money they had saved for the remainder of his fees.

On Thursday before Easter, Tusi went to the warden and asked if he could get some cleaning work from him and whether he would be allowed to stay in the hostel, as an overseas student from Savai'i, because of his situation.

"Tusi, overseas students are students from other countries excluding Samoa, so whichever island of Samoa you come from, you are still a local student", the warden explained.

"I am sorry sir. I had thought that once you leave home and cross any sea to attend this college, you would then be classified as an overseas student."

Fortunately, the kind warden considered Tusi to have misinterpreted the term 'overseas student', and therefore allowed him to stay on campus and gave him some lawn mowing work for the weekend. It was the first time in his life Tusi had been away from home at Easter. He was sad but courageous because he trusted God was with his parents and family and with him. Tusi went to church and was very happy.

After Easter, Tusi received a letter from his parents with some money to pay his fees but not the full amount required. His parents told Tusi that after selling their next copra harvest that was about to be dried, they would forward the rest of the fees. Tusi felt sad that his parents and family and grandma had to put in so much hard work to cover his fees when he couldn't be there to help them. With a thankful heart Tusi pushed aside his concerns about the potential consequences of his shortfall – that he would be sent home – and ran to the office to pay another partial instalment.

Before the secretary gave him a receipt for his money, she quietly told Tusi that the Head of School wanted to see him urgently. She knocked on the door, talked briefly with the Head of School, and asked Tusi to go in. Tusi took a few deep breaths and then calmly and slowly walked into the Head of School's office preparing himself for the word expulsion. Sweat started to soak into his clothes and his heart was beating at the speed of a runaway freight train.

The Head of School greeted Tusi with a handshake and asked him to sit down. "Why didn't you go home for Easter?" asked the principal.

"Sir, I did not have any money to pay my fare."

"I understand from the warden that you did some lawn mowing and cleaning, is that correct?"

"Yes sir."

"I also understand from the secretary that you still have to pay the rest of your fees, is that correct?"

"Yes sir", answered Tusi and tears started to well up in his eyes.

"Are you able to pay the rest of your fees today?"

"Sir, I received some money today from my parents, but I am still short. My parents have asked if I could be allowed to continue and they will try and pay the rest of my fees well before the end of semester."

The principal shook his head from side to side while closing his eyes momentarily. Then he stood up, extended his right hand to Tusi, and gave Tusi another handshake. "Don't cry, Tusi. You have done so well in school so far and I congratulate you. Keep on with the good work. Today, you have been awarded a scholarship from the government of New Zealand for the three years of your study at SPRCTA, well done."

As he profusely thanked the Head of School, tears fell freely from Tusi's eyes. The Head of School walked Tusi out and told the secretary to arrange all the paperwork for the scholarship award and to refund all payments previously made by Tusi.

With a thankful heart to God, Tusi wrote a letter to notify his parents of his scholarship. Tears of happiness splashed onto the page as Tusi wrote. He couldn't get the images of his parents and his grandma out of his mind as he kept singing in his heart the song 'The light in the darkness'.

Tusi scrolled through past events in his mind, especially the time his Grandma and parents were struggling in search of money for his fees. With great joy, he said to himself, "What a relief! However, this scholarship award came about I thank God, Grandma, my parents and family. Yes Grandma. Bright gleams the morning, Tusi, uplift the eye; Clouds and darkness disappearing, glory is nigh! Safe in the lifeboat, Tusi, sing, evermore, Glory, glory, hallelujah, Pull for the shore."

Tusi was glad when his friends returned to college after the Easter break and he could share his amazing news with them. His good friends Tana, Ken, Sauiluma and Alo celebrated Tusi's good fortune along with him.

"Congratulations Tusi. We are so happy to hear your good news. At least the greatest hurdle to your study is removed, well done friend", said Tana.

"You've done very well Tusi. I am so proud of you. I think it is time to celebrate your effort with another coffee and egg, don't you think so? But this time with a kettle you buy with your scholarship money", said Alo.

"Thanks, friends, for your support and help at all times. Yes Alo, we should have egg and coffee for celebration. Unfortunately, my scholarship money is just for the fees not to buy a kettle, but we can still use your multipurpose kettle my friend", said Tusi.

The scholarship award removed the worries and tension Tusi had had with regards to his college fees. Given the relief, Tusi then believed and accepted the fact that his failure or success in the college would totally depend on his own effort – nothing else. So, he promised himself he would try hard. To reinforce his positive thinking, Tusi recalled the interpretation of his dream by his uncle and the wise counsel of his grandma. "As water is vital to my body, honest continuous study is vital to my brain and I need courage to pursue that. This would be my goal – to pass all my exams giving fullness in happiness to my grandma, parents and family."

Tusi still considered himself to be an underdog and kept seeking help, asking questions and begging for explanations to solve difficulties in any subject from other students as well as Tana and Alo; and sought advice and counselling from the teaching staff on any subject matters he was in doubt of. As part of his commitment to study, Tusi refrained from the competitive sports he loved like rugby and football. Occasionally, Tusi would participate in table tennis for some exercise during short breaks after lunch and before dinner.

As time went by, Tusi found that he no longer was worried about and scared of tests and exams. His confidence in responding to emergency testing in any subject had greatly improved.

In 1971, Her Majesty Queen Elizabeth II and Prince Philip visited Samoa. The college hosted a morning tea for the royal visitors and Tusi was selected by the staff to represent the students at this special occasion. At the event Tusi had the opportunity to shake the hand of Her Majesty and to speak with her.

"It's a pleasure to meet you Tusi", said the Queen.

"It's a pleasure to meet Your Majesty."

"Had you heard of the Queen of London before our visit?"

"Your Majesty, when I was young, I learnt a song that started with 'Pussy cat pussy cat where have you been?' and the cat answered, 'I have been to London to visit the Queen'. That was the first time I heard about the Queen of London and I am glad that I don't have to go to London to shake your hand."

"You can still come and shake my hand if you have a chance to come to London."

"Certainly, your Majesty."

"I will look forward to you coming Tusi."

"Thank you, Your Majesty, and long live the Queen."

As result of his sustained efforts, Tusi won the first prize in his class every year of his three years in college and was named the student of the year when he graduated in 1971. Tusi believed that the ever-present help of God, the consistent positive guidance and support from his Grandma, parents and family, not to mention the stimulus from both negative actions and encouragements of friends, had helped transform each setback along his way into a step forward in his education and personal development.

Surely, Tusi reaped the benefit of what he had sown. The outcome of the true test of his obedience was fullness in happiness for himself and for his family. Mindful of his family's financial situation, Tusi didn't invite anyone from his family to his graduation. Instead, Tusi sent a letter to tell them the news that he was graduating from SPRCTA as student of the year and he asked them to say a prayer and sing the song 'Thanks be to God'.

Chapter Ten

Boars, bulls and taxi cabs

After graduation, Tusi stayed with his sister Fi and husband Lome in Apia while looking for a job. Because of competition, Tusi applied for any job that was advertised in the local newspaper regardless of field, location and pay. Unfortunately, Tusi was unsuccessful because other applicants had more experience and skills than him.

"How is the job search going, brother?" asked Fi.

"So far, I have failed all my job interviews because I don't have the experience like other interviewees."

"Yes brother, experience is one of the most important criteria in finding a job and it is a headache to students who have just finished school like you."

"You are certainly right. It's a pain. How in heaven I would get the experience and yet I spent the last three years in college? The only experience I have had was the practical work from the college besides the feeding of pigs and chicken when at home. So, what shall I do?"

"Just keep applying and keep trying."

As Tusi and his sister were discussing jobs, a government car drove by and stopped in front of the house. The driver was a senior veterinary officer and deputy head of the veterinary clinic of the Agriculture

Department located at the SPRCTA campus. He had been a supervisor of vet practical works when Tusi was in SPRCTA.

"Eh Tusi, is this your home?" asked the officer.

"Good morning Mau. Yes, this is our home. How are you?" said Tusi as he walked towards the car.

"I am very well thanking you. I am looking for the residence of Fau. Do you have any idea where it is?"

"Fau's home is directly behind our fence but you have to take that narrow track just behind that tree."

"Jump in. It's better if you can show me. Let's take a ride."

"What are you planning to do at Fau's home?"

"I have come to castrate the young boars for Fau because Ofe who was supposed to handle this job didn't come to work today."

"I can help you with that job if you want."

"I know you can handle castration with great confidence. Are you sure you can help out today?"

"Yes Mau. I am not doing anything special now besides discussing jobs with my sister, so I might as well help out to get some experience."

"That is great Tusi. You need experience to get a job nowadays. Okay, I'll let you handle the operation while I help hold the piglets in position. Just make sure you follow the normal procedure and ask if you can't remember how to do something."

On arrival, Mau introduced Tusi to Fau and his wife. Fau's wife was one of the recruitment officers for agricultural employees at the Public Service Commission.

"Yes, we know Tusi. He is our neighbour", said Fau.

"Tusi is now undertaking his field work in livestock science. He is going to be the surgeon today", declared Mau.

"I didn't know that Tusi was that good", said Fau's wife.

Within half an hour the surgery on the three suckling boars had been completed. Tusi handled the operation with great care for he knew that both Mau and his neighbours were assessing him. Tusi operated with the understanding that he would be blamed if something went wrong with the castration process. He showed the onlookers that he had the knowledge and experience to perform field veterinary work.

Fau and wife were surprised and amazed with the way Tusi handled the surgery. Mau too was very pleased and praised Tusi during the operation. As token of their appreciation afterwards, Fau and his wife offered Mau and Tusi a basket containing a roast leg of pork, two roast chickens and a basket of taros to take.

Before Mau and Tusi left, Tusi said to Fau and his wife, "Since I live next door, I would be happy to make regular visits to check on the piglets as their wounds heal, if you would allow me to."

"Please Tusi, come at any time. We certainly would welcome your help", said Fau's wife.

"You did very well Tusi. Are you good with castration of bulls too?" Fau asked. My brother on one of his rural plantations is looking for someone to castrate his bulls."

"Tusi is one of our best students who can handle castration of any kind of animal including bulls", interrupted Mau.

"Can I make arrangements for Tusi, through you, to come and castrate the young bulls on my brother's farm?"

"I think I have your brother's name on the program for next week and I will definitely take Tusi with me."

Tusi had no idea of what Mau was talking about in terms of work planning and arrangements. He just kept quiet, listened, contemplated and waited for an explanation from Mau.

As they left Fau's home, Mau said to Tusi, "You have done well my boy. Your timing was good and handling of your tools was excellent. I liked the way you made and cleaned the scrotal cuts of the piglets. Well done."

"I was very happy when I heard you saying that I am undertaking my field work as I definitely need some work experience in any available field."

"Yes. I knew you were a bit uncertain when I said that in front of Fau and wife. But you see, I wanted to show your neighbours, especially Fau's wife, that you could do the job. Fau's wife is a very influential lady and often involved in the selection panels for Government jobs. Secondly, there will be a vacancy for an assistant vet officer in our clinic very soon, a replacement for Ofe who will be leaving for New Zealand in two weeks' time. We will be looking for someone with knowledge, experience and skills. I think you have the knowledge, but you need to add to your experience and improve your skills. That is why I said to Fau and his wife that you are undertaking training now because you can work with me to get experience. However, you have to make a choice because you won't get paid any money for this work experience."

"I would not expect to be paid as long as I get the experience and improve my skills."

"Very good, Tusi. That is the sacrifice you must make. You won't get paid with money but as you saw today you may receive free food at times when you visit and help farmers."

"Mau, food is great pay to me anyway."

"I will speak with my boss this afternoon and let him know that you are undertaking some work experience without pay with me. So, as from tomorrow, I can help by picking you up and bringing you home every day, for the next two or three weeks. I want you to show my boss not only that you have the interest, but you also have the competency in rural livestock extension. Given your good work today Tusi, you can take the basket of food from Fau because I don't have any money to pay you."

Respecting the senior officer, Tusi responded, "No Mau. You take the food. All I want from you is more chances to work for some experience. I am looking forward to serving and working with you from tomorrow."

"Thanks for your help Tusi. By the way, don't forget to go and check out Fau's piglets when you have time this afternoon."

Tusi loved his job training with Mau. Every day, he brought home some food from farmers he worked for. This was a great help to his family and especially his brother-in-law who enjoyed consuming fried testicle meat as he drank his beer.

When the vacancy for an assistant veterinary officer for the Vet Clinic at SPRCTA was advertised, Tusi applied immediately and was called in for an interview. Tusi was selected for the position, apparently because of his experience and competency from his job training with Mau as witnessed by Fau's wife who was one of the members of the interview panel.

Tusi received his first fortnight's pay on a Wednesday. That night, there was a big gathering in their home as many friends and relatives came together to pray for one of the old ladies of the family who was sick and dying. Traditionally, the host family would prepare food and drinks for whoever came, invited or uninvited. This was a challenging and expensive responsibility for the host family. Now that he was a working member of the family, Tusi was expected to assist with the expenses. Tusi gave extra money to his sister who organised the night. He also gave money to the pastor and chiefs and some of the old people who were present. Because the relatives and friends were praising Tusi about his job and the good pay he received, he responded a little too openhandedly. Consequently, when Tusi woke up the next morning his wallet was completely empty, and he had nothing left in the bank.

On Friday night of the same week, one of Tusi's uncles from one of the rural villages came to Fi and her family begging for some money to buy ten cases of tinned *eleni* fish to pay a fine for his son who had been involved in a fight with the son of the pastor over plantation boundaries. When Fi asked Tusi to contribute a donation, he told her that the pay he had received two days earlier was all gone. At the end of the discussion, Tusi borrowed some money from his sister and her husband to contribute to repaying the fine. He promised to repay the loan when he received his next pay.

Early the next morning, Pepelo another aunty of Tusi, came with two fine mats to Fi and her husband to exchange them for some money to pay her fare to travel to the funeral of her sister on the island of Savai'i. Again, Tusi spoke with Fi and her husband regarding a contribution.

"Sister, I really have no money. My pay has gone including the money I put aside for my parents and grandma. I already borrowed two hundred talas (T$200.00) from you yesterday so what could I possibly give? If you like, and Pepelo agrees, I can take the mats and sell them to a shop", said Tusi.

Pepelo supported the idea, trusting Tusi would make a good bargain to meet her demand.

Tusi walked for about one kilometre to the shop in the nearby village near the waterfall pool. At the counter of the shop was a beautiful lady doing some bookkeeping while listening to the radio. Before the lady said a word, Tusi noticed the name Mele Paga written on the face of the radio.

"*Talofa* (hallo) what can I do for you?" asked the lady.

"Good morning Mele, nnnn."

"Man, how do you know my name?" asked the lady.

"Well it isn't hard to know the names of beautiful ladies like you. You look just as beautiful as one of the girls I went to school with."

"What is her name?"

At that moment a slim lady wearing a mini skirt and a tightly fitting top poked her head through the back door and called, "Who is there Mele?"

Instead of answering, Mele asked Tusi again, "Man, what is her name?"

As Tusi was saying the name Miss Paga, the mini skirted lady walked in towards the counter. When she saw Tusi she lifted her hands as trying to affirm her view of the customer, jumped on the counter, slid over to where Tusi was standing, and threw her body at Tusi. As Tusi caught her, she hugged him and kissed his checks saying, "Tusi, how are you? How are you my dear friend? How did you get here at this early hour of the day? Long time no see! What a morning Tusi!" said Aiga.

Tusi and Aiga then took a few minutes to reminisce about the things they had done together while at school in Pouli.

In the meanwhile, Aiga had taken over from Mele who looked a bit jealous but could not say a word because Aiga was the older of the two.

"What is this sack, Tusi?"

"Look Aiga, I am a bit embarrassed, but I really need some money for one of my aunties. This aunty whom I had never seen before arrived at my sister's house very early this morning with these fine mats begging for money so she can travel to a family funeral. So, I came here to try and sell the mats. What a coincidence that I find my good friend here! Do you buy and sell these things?"

"Don't worry Tusi, I will give you sixty talas (T$60.00) to give your aunty and I will give you the rest of the price when you come and see me tonight okay?"

"Oh, what a relief! Thank you Aiga. You're such a great friend as always. How will I repay your great assistance Aiga?"

"Don't mention it Tusi, just make sure you come tonight, and we will talk some more okay?"

"What time Aiga?"

"Any time after work and send Mele to get me if I am not in the shop."

Tusi went home and gave Pepelo the $60.00. Even though the money was less than Pepelo had expected she had no choice but to accept the money with thanks to Tusi, Fi and Lome. After Pepelo left, Tusi had a conversation with Fi and Lome while Lome enjoyed his weekend beer.

"You know Fi and Lome, I had never seen these uncles and aunties of ours in the past and now they come to borrow money. I never saw these relatives when our parents and family were struggling trying to find some money for our school fees and see they are the first people to come and borrow and so on", complained Tusi.

"Brother, that is our life in Samoa. We live for the extended families, the culture, and religion. At difficult times, you would normally struggle with your immediate family but when harvest times come the extended families, culture and religion will be your closest friends. This is a bit hard to digest because we spend more of our income on extended relatives, cultural and religious activities than on our immediate family. It is the way we live and unfortunately we have to deal with it."

"Sister, I am broke and already in debt. I even spent the amount of money I left aside for my parents and grandma and I didn't even buy something for myself with my first pay. Now before the next pay comes my wage will be insufficient to pay what I borrowed, oh what a life! Sister, I hope no more relatives will come to borrow more money because I will give them stones instead", complained Tusi.

"Brother there may be no more relatives coming but you have to think about tomorrow."

"What about tomorrow sister?"

"Well tomorrow at church there will be a special donation for the poor in developing countries and a monthly donation for the pastor and his family and also a donation for youth development", explained Fi.

"Sister, what will I donate for the poor in those countries if I am poor already, do you want me to borrow again? What do you think Lome?"

Before Lome opened another stubby he slowly replied, "Brother Tusi, don't borrow to donate. Donate only what you have. If you don't have money, tell God that you can't donate. Of course, before you even tell God, He knows that you don't have anything to donate and He is very pleased because you are honest. Donating borrowed money is not good in many ways."

"How?" asked Fi.

"Okay, first, if Tusi, a poor boy, borrowed for a donation, he will increase his debt, but his pay won't increase when he borrows? Second, if Tusi, a poor boy, borrows to donate, he is donating somebody else's money – not his own money – and so on", replied Lome.

"Lome you shouldn't worry because our relatives overseas send us money, which we can use to pay our loans", commented Fi.

"That is a very sad situation at least to me, my dear. From the bottom of my heart I thank overseas relatives for their help because without their genuine financial assistance most if not all locals will starve. The hidden disgrace that the locals don't feel is that most of our overseas relatives are struggling just like us because they also borrow money themselves. They pay high rents and enormous bills but because we keep asking for money, they then force themselves to borrow – and that is not good because at the end of the process our relatives overseas and us will still be poor because we all borrow", explained Lome as Fi was still pressing her donation argument.

"Lome, as you very well know, it is a shame to a family if we don't donate or donate very little in church, so we can't ignore these donations because people can talk and surely you don't want to hear them mocking us", said Fi.

"Ha ha Fi, I call that stupidity. I know that a lot of people donate not because of love for the poor but of shame for donating little or nothing in front of people. People like you donate more than you have – more than we have – because you want people to see and hear about your big donation and praise your name and yet when you come home you are stressed and worried about how to cover our own expenses. My dear wife, you go to church to praise God for what he gave you through the work of your own hands to donate, not to receive praise from people because you donated what you have borrowed from someone else – do you agree brother?" Lome said while laughing and opening another bottle of beer.

"My dear husband, if you are so concerned with donations for the poor, why don't you stop drinking and donate your beer money for the poor?"

"Ha ha my dear wife, my beer money is my pay to myself. I had to pay me for working so hard for the money I give you to donate to whoever you want in or out of church. When that money is gone, you don't ask me for any more until the next payday because you know I don't borrow. Secondly my dear, I don't sacrifice my beer money for an extra donation for the poor overseas because I understand that only a fraction of donations for the poor reach the poor. If I were correct, then, why would I sacrifice my pay, for the sake of the joy of evil interventions? What do you think brother?" said Lome laughing.

"Well Lome, I think you are right because you have to pay yourself. But brother, would you sacrifice your beer money to buy food for your starving children if that was the only available money in the family?" asked Tusi.

"My dear brother that is a different topic – that is called sacrificing one donation for another, given the validity of the reason. Who am I to keep donating for my beer and yet my children are dying! My gift from God is my children and it is my responsibility to feed my children to honour God. In that case, I would sacrifice my beer money to feed my dying children", explained Lome.

"So Lome, what should I do if I need to donate without borrowing and I don't get that much from my job", asked Tusi.

Lome replied, "My dear brother, if you still want to donate given your insufficient income, my advice is not to borrow but look for an additional job."

Taking Lome's advice seriously, Tusi pondered the idea of a second job. But what, how and where to get another job was the problem. While thinking of a way to get another job, Tusi remembered Aiga's invitation to visit in the evening to talk some more about their past days at school. Tusi then made sure he would not miss the invitation.

When Tusi arrived at the shop, Mele was serving customers and Aiga was packing something in the car.

Mele asked, "Tusi can you please help me to lift this box for Aiga?"

"I'll take it for you."

To Aiga's surprise, Tusi came out with the box as she was arranging things in the boot of the car. "Oh, thanks Tusi, you came right on time."

"What do you mean?"

"Well you and I are going for a drive to my aunty's house in a minute and we will most likely be spending the night there."

"What do you mean?"

"Look, stop asking questions and get these things in the boot so we can go. I will explain along the way. Can you drive?"

"No, I can't."

"Okay, don't worry I will teach you how."

Aiga and Tusi drove along the beach road before stopping at a small restaurant to pick up a few plates of food. They then drove on past the government complexes and the main national hospital and headed up the mountain range. At the top of the mountain, Aiga turned into a very narrow and rough dirt road. Winding up the side of the hill, they travelled about another kilometre into the bush until Tusi saw a gate ahead. As they approached the gate fixed between two large mango trees, four dogs raced out to greet them. Barking alongside, the dogs escorted them until Aiga parked the car underneath a leafy mango tree.

"Where are we Aiga?"

"We are at the home of my aunty. She left yesterday for a week's holiday in New Zealand and she asked me to look after the house and feed her dogs, cats and chickens. So, that is my job for the whole week, and I can stay here or work from home if I want. As for tonight, we can spend the night here if you like."

After unpacking a few things from the car, Tusi helped Aiga feed the animals. She then walked Tusi around the gardens, picking a few ripe bananas from bunches hanging on the trees as they went. Then they went inside the house and made their way up to the front balcony on the top floor, which overlooked the town and harbour of Apia.

"What a fantastic view!" exclaimed Tusi.

"Yes, and what a hot afternoon, I am so thirsty. What about you Tusi?"

"Yes, it is hot – a cold drink would be nice."

"What would you like to drink, Tusi?"

"You know I don't drink alcohol so a glass of coke would do for me if you don't mind."

Aiga fixed a rum and coke for herself and added about half a teaspoon of rum to Tusi's glass of coke. "Cheers Tusi", said Aiga lifting her glass to touch Tusi's glass.

"Cheers", said Tusi, lifting his glass.

"Bottoms up for a special drink for a special long-time friend", said Aiga.

"Yes, bottoms up and many thanks for the invitation from a very special long-time friend", replied Tusi and both quickly emptied their glasses.

"That coke tasted great Aiga."

"Do you want some more?"

"I don't mind."

After a few drinks, the two were still enjoying the evening warm breeze and the moonlight while admiring the night view of the town with its background of the vast Pacific Ocean.

"So Tusi, did you say you haven't driven a car before?"

"I wish I could drive but I don't have a car."

"Well, as promised, I am going to teach you how to drive. Knowing you, I don't think you will find learning to drive difficult but from my experience driving is an unnecessary evil if you don't enjoy it. Knowing how to drive is very different from enjoying driving so I promise I will make sure you both know how to drive and enjoy driving", Aiga said as she fixed another round of rum and coke for both. "You know, there are automatic and manual cars. If you know how to drive a manual car, driving an automatic is easy but you can't drive a manual with only automatic driving experience. So, I am going to teach you how to drive a manual car."

"Oh, that is what I was hoping for Aiga."

Tusi started to feel energetic, unaware that Aiga had been adding a small amount of rum to his coke. "But how can you teach me to drive while drinking alcohol?"

"My dear Tusi, I think a bit of rum helps to energise me as I explain and demonstrate driving techniques as we go along. I think you too should try a taste of rum so that you can enjoy learning while practicing. Give me your class. I'll put in just a tiny drop of rum for you to taste", said Aiga as she added more rum.

Because he had been unknowingly drinking coke with a dash of rum from the start, Tusi didn't notice any difference. "Thanks, Aiga, but it tastes just like a normal coke. Can you put in another drop please?"

In a little while, given the warm breeze and the sound of music in the open forest, Tusi and Aiga were enjoying themselves as they prepared for the driving lesson. Tusi lifted Aiga and called to no one, "Long live my instructor and long live the driver."

Unfortunately, given the excess amount of rum he had consumed, Tusi flopped on the sofa and gone.

The crow of the roosters at dawn woke Aiga. Opening her eyes, she saw the shiny eyes of a cat sitting on the chair by the couch she was lying.

"Tusi, Tusi, it is daytime."

"Nnnnn did I pass my driving test?" asked a sobered Tusi.

"You got an A grade, but more practice may give you an AA", replied Aiga.

In their conversation, Tusi told Aiga that he really needed a second job for some extra money. "Well now you know how to drive what about driving a taxi, say two hours before work and a couple of hours after work."

"I wouldn't mind that, but I don't know whether I am qualified, and I don't know where to get a taxi driving job."

"Honey, I am currently working in the Bank of Western Samoa (BWS) and at the same time looking after the management of our four taxis. Now one of our taxis is available. Would you like to try?"

"Wait Aiga, did you say you are managing four taxis?"

"That is right. Does that surprise you?"

"Definitely Aiga. So, besides the shop you also manage four taxis? That is a big responsibility. Four taxis? That is called rich. I wish I had a rich family like yours Aiga. You have a blessed family honey, well done. But are you sure and confident about my driving experience?"

"From the way you drove I think you have the basics skills. Just be careful with the clutch and speed, that's all. How about coming here for lunch after church today and then we can do more practice?"

"You are the instructor and the owner, so whatever you say I follow."

Before driving Tusi home, Aiga gave Tusi one hundred tala, the rest of the price of the two fine mats, and an extra $50 to help Tusi with his offering difficulty.

After arriving home, Tusi started the *umu* (cooking) straight away just before Fi and Lome woke up. He moved quickly to clean and make sure everything was in good order to ensure nothing would delay him from his special lunch and his interview for a second job.

Before preparing to go to church, Tusi gave his sister and Lome $WS50.00 to assist in the offering for the poor in the developing countries, $WS50.00 for the offering of the pastor and $WS50.00 for the youth development.

"Brother where did you get this money from?" asked Fi.

"My friend who owns the shop that I sold the two mats to, gave me some money last night. She said that she had underpriced the mats by that much, so we might as well use the money as a donation, what do you think Lome?" asked Tusi.

"Good idea Tusi, it's not our money so why keep it. The *papalagi* (white people) gave the money for the brown people to give. All is okay with me", replied Lome.

After church, Tusi told Fi that he would not have lunch at home because he had to go for an interview for a second job and have lunch with a friend. Fi prepared a small basket of food for Tusi to take and reminded him to try to come back in time for the evening service. In the meantime, Tusi was chatting with Lome while Lome had his second bottle of beer.

"So, what sort of second job you are going for brother?" asked Lome.

"I don't know brother and I don't care so long as I can get a job that gives extra money to help with our family affairs."

"Remember, I told you that I can teach you how to drive a taxi whenever you are ready brother", said Lome as a new white sedan drove in and parked in front of the house. A slim lady dressed in a white mini and wearing a white church hat opened the door, jumped out, and walked towards the house where Lome and Tusi sitting.

"Tusi I know that lady. She is a daughter of one of the members of the Legislative Assembly. She has lots of money and owns a few shops. She knows me well because my job is to fix their taxis everyday including weekends if there's an accident. She is probably coming to get me to fix one of their taxis, we'll see", said Lome. As Lome spoke Tusi got up, combed his hair, tightened his belt, and walked over to greet Aiga.

"Hi Lome, are you enjoying your weekend drink?" Aiga called before greeting Tusi.

"Good morning Aiga, how is everything? Any problem with the taxis?"

"No, everything is running well. I am here to pick up Tusi. Are you related Lome?" inquired Aiga.

"Tusi is the best brother of my wife Fi. So, he is my brother-in-law who normally does incredible things that only pretty ladies like Aiga could understand and admire", answered Lome.

"Thank you Lome. You have put me on the top of Mt Vaea and probably your brother-in-law will lift me even higher to the top of Mt Silisili, isn't that right Tusi?" joked Aiga.

Before Tusi and Aiga left, Aiga accepted a glass of beer from Lome and told Lome she would bring a box of beer for him when she brought Tusi home.

"Tusi, are you ready? You will have to drive us from here while I hold the food okay?"

Lome interrupted, "But Tusi doesn't know how to drive Aiga."

"Don't worry Lome. I gave him a very good test last night and if he does well today, he can start driving our new sedan taxi tonight."

"Are you kidding me Aiga?"

"No, I am telling you the truth, Tusi deserves a second job. He is a very good and fast driver, but he needs more practice with the clutch and to learn how and when to stop."

"Yes, Tusi is a fellow who doesn't know the word stop, he is a workaholic not an alcoholic like me ha ha", laughed Lome as he waved goodbye.

Given his good performance Tusi managed to win the trust of Aiga in his driving. Aiga gave Tusi her new sedan taxi to keep and drive at anytime suitable when he was not working at his normal everyday job. As an additional bonus, Tusi had a permanent booking fare to pick up his instructor every evening for a ride to the mountain house to feed the animals.

To accommodate his two jobs, Tusi woke up at about 4.30 am and drove the taxi until he started his main job at 8 am. During his main job's lunch break, from 12.00 to 1.00 pm, Tusi drove the taxi. After work, he drove the taxi again from 4.30 pm until 11.00 pm every night from Monday to Friday. On Saturdays, Tusi drove the taxi for the whole day, and he rested on Sundays.

When he started his taxi job, most people thought that Tusi was married to Aiga because not only did he keep the taxi with him all the time, but he also seemed to be a permanent driver for Aiga every day. On Sundays especially, Aiga loved to take Tusi with her to church so that people could see them together doing things like a married couple. They would share the Bible, the hymnbook and at offering times, Aiga and Tusi would walk up and donate money together.

On the third week of his new job, one-night Tusi ran into a free-ranging and quite sizeable pig on the road, which forced the taxi off the road and into a coconut tree. The whole front of the car was smashed and Tusi escaped death with only a cut on his forehead and bruises on his left arm and shoulder.

As a result of pleas from Aiga, her father did not charge Tusi for the damage but stopped Tusi from diving his taxis. Tusi was thankful for the leniency of the decision.

"Sorry Aiga for what has happened. I was a bit tired and I could hardly see the road because of the rain."

"It's okay honey. Dad understands. That's why he didn't ask for any payment but stopped you from driving."

"Do you think I will be allowed to drive again?"

"Oh yes, darling. Once you recover, I will speak to my dad and ask him for another chance but for the time being I will pick you up every morning and after work, okay?" encouraged Aiga.

Chapter Eleven

The call

Two weeks after he lost his second job, Tusi was called in to see the Head of School of SPRCTA on a Wednesday afternoon. Tusi was unsettled wondering if he had done something wrong in his veterinary job. Maybe he had spent fewer hours at his main job while he was driving the taxi? Or maybe a second job like taxi driving was not allowed? Or was it something related to the accident? Whatever the reason for his summons, Tusi prepared for the worst.

In their urgent meeting, there was no time for casual conversation. The principal informed Tusi that he had been awarded a scholarship from the United Nations to study for a Bachelor of Agricultural Science at the University of the West Indies in Trinidad. Furthermore, Tusi would need to leave for Trinidad on the coming Sunday. Tusi was speechless. He couldn't see himself getting ready to leave for overseas at such short notice. And what about his family? He would need to inform and farewell his parents, his grandma and the rest of the family. Speechless, Tusi could do little but stare in wonder at the Head of School and to try and take in the instructions he was providing.

After the meeting, Tusi went and sat alone inside one of the laboratories for a couple of minutes trying to comprehend the news. Closing his eyes, Tusi silently meditated his favorite Psalm 23. He silently thanked God, the Head of School and the United Nations for the opportunity provided, his parents, Grandma and his relatives and friends for their support, and himself for whatever he had done to get the scholarship award.

In his mind Tusi answered, "Yes, thanked God, my parents and grandma will have the money supply while I would be away for 3 years – I just don't believe this Lord. I will be getting free education, travelling and meet new people, see new countries for free – what a great security and great blessing. This surprised call is totally a blessing – thank God. I'll go."

Tusi accepted the award and because he didn't have any other choice, he promised to himself that despite the short time frame nothing would stop him from meeting the guidelines and instructions as provided. With that decision made, Tusi was more than happy to start preparing for this next major step in his life. Instead of blowing his own trumpet, he decided to keep the news a secret. But he soon discovered that his news had started to filter out through college contacts.

"Hey Tusi, I heard the news from the secretary of the college. Is it true?" Tana asked.

"Friend, I don't know what to say. I am still shock from the news. I just didn't believe something like this would happen to me."

"I congratulate you boy. This is a special and rare opportunity. Does anybody else know besides the secretary and me?"

"I haven't told anyone else but, as you know, sometimes the spread of news in our small country is faster than any hurricane. Preferably, I really would like to keep my going overseas a secret."

"Why?"

"Because I don't want to go through an emotional farewell with my friends and family. Given this short notice, wouldn't it be better if I just get on the plane, fly away and go ahead with the mission without emotional drawbacks? It is just a wish but then again some people would consider that to be disrespectful."

For the rest of Wednesday afternoon, Tana and Tusi were inseparable because both young men had the feeling of missing each other already. They went together to various government and non-government offices to make sure Tusi completed all the required documentation for his trip.

Before Tusi went home after work, the secretary gave Tusi an envelope saying, "Here's a letter from Aiga. She dropped in at about 2.30 pm to see you but you were in town at that time with Tana. She told me to tell you that she cannot pick you up this afternoon because she and her parents had to catch the last ferry to Savai'i."

Tusi went and sat under the fig tree by the administration building, opened the letter and read:

To my honey Tusi,

I was trying to contact you after lunch today to tell of the great news: OUR PLAN IS APPROVED.

My parents finally accepted my request to marry you, the man I love. Since our agreement last week to start a family, I spoke with my parents. Dad was very impressed, but Mum was uncertain about my behaviour until this morning. During our lunch today, Dad and Mum gave me their full support for our plan to get married.

My parents suggested that our wedding should take place before they leave for holidays in America early next month so that we can then look after our businesses. I accepted my parents' suggestion on your behalf. I told my parents that we are ready at any time and the quicker the better. I just can't wait honey.

According to my parents our wedding is going to be a big one involving the culture and religion – nothing small like signing the documents in the Post Office as you suggested last week. Because my parents are so excited, they decided that they and I should take a trip to alert our extended families in Savai'i and discuss the wedding program. We leave for Savai'i this afternoon and should be back on early Sunday morning in time for the church service.

Please accept my parents' invitation for Sunday lunch so that we could finalise the date and program of our wedding. Take care.

I love you honey,

Aiga.

Tusi reread the letter a few times and said to himself, "What is this Lord! I have just made up my mind on a sudden call to go overseas and now this unexpected news about the wedding. How could this wedding plan and this scholarship come around at the same time? I could have had the wedding last week, or the beginning of this week before going overseas on Sunday. But again, if that was to happen there could have been a lot of difficulties if the scholarship conditions wouldn't allow Aiga to come with me. I cannot reject the scholarship for the sake of the wedding. The wedding can be postponed until some other time in future. But then again, Trinidad is so far away. I would need a lot of money to come back for the wedding. What if Aiga could come over and we could get married in Trinidad? That would be great but again expenses would also be great. I wish I knew this scholarship news yesterday or the wedding approval news before my urgent meeting with the Head of School today. What a mishmash!

And Aiga has already left for Savai'i without the slightest idea at all my plans and program up to Sunday. I can't even contact her because there are no telephones. If only she had given me details of her whereabouts in Savai'i. Then I could have tried to catch up when I go to Savai'i on Friday, to let her know about my trip and to talk with her parents about what to do regarding the wedding. What a life! A total mishmash!"

As Tusi was about to go home, Tana passed by and asked, "You look very concerned Tusi. What time is Aiga picking you up?"

"She isn't coming because she and her parents left this afternoon to go to Savai'i."

"That fits in well with my plan, Tusi. You see, for the last time I want to go to the cinema with you tonight. Is that okay with you?"

"That is not a problem, but…"

"But what? You still prefer to go with Aiga instead?"

"No, it is nothing to do with that. You know Tana, about five minutes ago, the secretary handed me this letter from Aiga. Have a read and tell me what you think."

After reading the letter a couple of times, Tana was quiet for a moment before he said, "I know you are very close with Aiga and this is not an easy matter."

"Yes Tana. I don't know, Aiga is a lovely lady and I respect her to be my future wife, if I can say that now."

"Tusi my best friend, just keep your cool and think properly. This is a matter of loving Aiga or your parents. We often shared about our parents. The common wish of our parents is for opportunities for further studies not opportunities to get married. If you are honest with your love for your parents, then I am sure you know the answer to Aiga's letter."

Before Tusi spoke Tana continued, "My friend, there is a lot of time in the future to arrange marriages but there is only one opportunity to be called for a scholarship. Who knows, this could be the one and only chance you get to study for a degree that is fully paid for. Probably only one in so many millions of people would get this kind of opportunity." As encouragement Tana continued, "My friend, girls are plentiful under coconut trees. You can just flick your fingers and they come like hungry fish. Anyway, the decision is yours."

"Thanks, Tana, for your brotherly advice. You reminded me of what my mother stressed when I was in doubt of going to Pouli. Opportunity comes just once, and when it comes, I must make use of it or I will miss it forever."

"Keep that in your mind, my friend."

"Tana, I had already made up my mind and committed to go for further study before I received Aiga's letter. So, after reading the letter and debating the situation in my mind, I found no reason to abandon going overseas this Sunday. However, I am just trying to find a better way to explain what is happening so that Aiga and her parents understand my decision when they receive the news."

"That is a brave decision brother. I am proud of you. Remember your grandma's favourite song! Leave the poor old stranded wreck and pull for the shore. We will sing and discuss some more after the pictures tonight."

On Thursday, Tusi went shopping for his trip overseas, and for gifts for his parents and family. For his trip overseas, he bought a new suitcase with only a few items knowing that he would buy more overseas.

For the farewell trip to his family, Tusi bought another new suitcase for his parents; a white shirt, a tie and a black *ie lavalava* for his dad; a white dress and a hat for his mother to wear to church; new dresses and thongs for his sisters; new pairs of sandals for his brother and his wife; and sweets for the children. For his grandma, Tusi bought a small white bag to keep her Bible and hymn book, a small necklace with a tiny wooden cross, a white dress and a white hat to wear to church.

Aware that he would not be seeing his home again for a long time, Tusi looked upon his farewell as a very big event. In his mind his farewell was to give special thanks to God led by the pastor and wife; to thank his parents, grandma, family and friends for their support with his education; and to give some gifts to his grandma, parents, family and friends. Because of the large amount of money, he now possessed Tusi decided to buy two tins of *pisupo* (weighing about six pounds each) for the farewell, leaving enough cash left over in case his parents wanted something else during the farewell.

"What are these two new large suitcases?" asked his sister Fi.

Wanting to keep everything about his trip secret, Tusi replied, "They belong to my friend and he asked me if he can keep one suitcase in our house for the weekend and take the other one with us tonight for his family in Savai'i."

"Oh, where are you going?"

"My friend asked me to go to Savai'i for the weekend to visit his family and at the same time see our family. If things work out well, we may be back on Saturday evening."

"That is a very quick trip. Do you have money to pay your fare and to buy something for Mum and Dad and Grandma?"

"Oh yes, I borrowed enough money from my friend. Take this money to pay back what I had borrowed from you and Lome", said Tusi, making sure all his debts were settled.

"Thanks brother. Are you sure you have enough?"

"Don't worry sister. I have more than enough."

"Well, send my love to Dad and Mum, Grandma and the rest of the family, and come back safe."

Very early Friday morning Tusi travelled to the island of Savai'i. He took the bus to Fanua wharf, the ferry across to Loga wharf and another bus to his village. On Loga wharf, Tusi met his old-time friend Fou who was waiting for his sisters Su and Sieni to pick him up.

"Hey Tusi, how are you? Are you coming home or going to Apia?"

"Fou my friend, I'm fine and I am coming home. How are you? I haven't seen you for a while."

"I am fine Tusi. Gosh you look fresh and smart and well and so on. Sieni is at home too. She came yesterday to collect some mats for her school fair."

"How are Sieni and Su?"

"They are well. They are coming to pick me up in our new pickup, would you like a lift home?"

"Thanks for the offer but I have to do some shopping before catching the last bus."

"But that bus normally arrives late evening, usually at devotion time?"

"That is perfect timing because I don't want to rush in case, I miss something."

"How long are you home for?"

"Just for tonight."

"Why so short?"

"Look Fou, my short visit is an urgent one and nobody, not even my parents, know I am coming. Since you are my best friend, I can tell you providing you remain silent until I see you tonight."

"Come on Tusi, you know very well that I would always keep your secrets, I promise."

"Okay, I am coming to say farewell to my parents, family and friends because I am leaving on Sunday for school overseas."

"Tusi that is a big, a very big thing."

"As I said before, nobody knows except you, so please keep it secret. I will see you tonight."

"But my parents should know because the job of the *faife'au* is to conduct the farewell service of anybody leaving the village – especially in the case of going overseas, and boy for a long time!"

"Okay, do me a favour, my friend. Please don't let my parents or anybody else know except for Reverend Maka and his wife. But please wait until say about half an hour before the bell rings for the evening devotion of the village before you tell your parents, okay? Promise?"

"Okay, I promise, but isn't that leaving it too late to tell my parents?"

"No, I think that is the perfect time because the bus normally arrives about that time, or better still, wait until the bus arrives and then tell your parents." Tusi gave Fou $WS10.00 and invited him and sisters to come to his farewell.

"I will wait for you my friend."

On their drive home, Fou could not resist sharing the news with his sisters. They were amazed and sad for they would miss their friend. Respecting Tusi, they all agreed that nobody would say a word until they met Tusi that night. Without the knowledge of their parents, Fou and his sisters each prepared a small gift as a surprise for Tusi when he arrived.

Half an hour before the bell rang for the village devotion, Fou who was doing the cooking with Su and Sieni in their cooking hut, saw Tusi's mother enter their house and have a short word with their father (Pastor Maka) and their mother.

"Su and Sieni, I think the parents of Tusi must have got the news about Tusi from some other source", said Fou.

"Why do you say that?" asked Su.

"Tusi's mother has just left after a short word with Dad and Mum", replied Fou.

"That's okay, we'll wait and see", said Su.

"Shall I ask Mum?" asked Sieni.

"No, just pretend we don't know anything. Just get your flowers ready and watch out for the time the bus arrives. When the bus arrives in front of their house, we will surprise Tusi with our gifts before going into the house", suggested Fou.

"That is a good idea. We can all walk Tusi inside and join the farewell devotion", agreed Su.

Pastor Maka and wife dressed up in white as they normally did when they visited families for special devotions and cultural occasions. Maka took a few minutes to read his Bible in preparation for the service while Fa'apito prepared a bouquet of flowers to take with them. Ten minutes before the bell rang Fa'apito called out to Su, Sieni and Fou, "We are going to the Pau family for devotions. Say a prayer when the bell rings and look after the house. We may be a little late for dinner."

When the pastor and his wife arrived, the house of Pau was packed with relatives and friends of the family. The parents of Lei, the parents of Sega, chief Lata and his wife, chief Tala, Pulu and his wife, among others were all present. Reverend Maka and his wife walked around shaking hands with the people who sat in a circle, before they settled in the front. After a few words of welcome and greetings, Reverend Maka got himself ready with his Bible and hymn book while all those gathered waited for the bell for the service to start. In the meantime, the bus had stopped in front of the house of Pau, which was set back about 50 yards from the road. Because they were about to start the devotion, nobody came out to check who was arriving by bus.

From inside the bus Tusi saw that his parents' house was brightly lit with two lanterns and was full of people. As he alighted from the bus, the passengers called out goodbye to him. Before the bus moved on, Fou, Su and Sieni welcomed Tusi with flower laces around his neck and hugged and kissed him.

"Okay folks, thanks for waiting for me and a special thanks for your gifts. We'll have a good talk afterwards but let us go into the house and meet everyone there, for the devotion will be starting soon", said Tusi with a peacock feeling and trying to think of what to say on meeting whoever was waiting in the full house.

"Yes, good idea, the devotion bell will be ringing soon. Tusi, just wait a second here with the girls and I'll take your suitcase in and be back quickly to help you carry in your heavy box", Fou said.

After Fou dropped the suitcase by Tusi's sister, the pastor called Fou to come and sit by his side. Maka whispered in Fou's ear, "Who is coming?"

"Dad, Tusi is coming to say farewell because he is leaving on Sunday for school overseas. He told me that he is leaving tomorrow morning for Apia", Fou whispered back.

"Who is at the bus with Tusi?"

"Su and Sieni."

"Go and tell Tusi and the girls to come through the front not the back of the house."

"Okay Dad."

Fou ran and passed on to Tusi and the girls the instructions from the pastor (entering from the front of the house, especially when the chiefs and pastor and people are already settled in the house, is very unusual in the Samoan culture – only people of authority like the pastor and chiefs can make alterations to these cultural conventions). As they walked towards the house, the devotion bell rang. It stopped ringing just as Tusi entered the front door. The pastor stood up, hugged Tusi for few seconds and said, "Welcome son. Congratulations and be brave during your farewell."

His wife stood up, hugged and kissed Tusi and said, "Welcome Tusi and be brave."

The chiefs and their wives got up, hugged, kissed and comforted Tusi to be brave. Moving from person to person, Tusi received the same encouragement to be brave. At the very core of his heart he wanted to greet his parents and grandma.

"Yes Mum, how are you? I love you Mum. Don't cry Mum, I am here, thank God", Tusi said.

"Hi son. I love you and be brave", replied Kika as she hugged and kissed her son.

"Hi Dad. How are you? I missed you so much Dad", said Tusi while hugging his dad who was in tears.

"Hi son. How did you know?"

"Know what Dad?"

It took a few seconds before Pau said, "Be brave son."

"Dad don't cry. I am here and I am brave", said Tusi while tightly hugging his dad.

"I want to have a long talk with you and Mum after the devotion. I love you Dad, let me see Grandma, where is she?" said Tusi while Pau kept holding Tusi tightly. Turning his head trying to locate Grandma, Tusi saw behind the people who were sitting in a circle, a fine mat covered with a white sheet and flowers on the top. Taking hold of his dad's arms Tusi asked, "Dad where is Grandma?" There was no answer. As Tusi repeated his question he was wetted with his dad's tears. There was still no answer except for a tight cuddle from his dad. Tusi's mother separated Tusi from his dad, cuddled Tusi close and walked him over to meet Grandma. "Oh no. Grandma no. No Grandma. I am here and you go, no, no, Grandma. Couldn't you wait Grandma? No, Grandma no", Tusi mourned, kissing, talking and calling to the dead body of his grandma who had passed away two hours before his arrival.

On hearing the twenty-one peals of the devotion bell ringing out through the quiet of the evening, the people of the village knew that somebody had passed away. People could tell the location of the family of the dead person by the presence of the *faife'au* and his wife for the devotion. Tusi's arrival caused a delay in the start of the service at the Pau family. By the time their service started, all the other families around them had finished their own devotions and the people crowded at Pau's house to find out the news. The house was soon full to overflowing, so many ended up standing around the house listening to the service.

After a few hymns and the Bible reading, the pastor spoke. "The title of my sermon tonight is 'The Happy Farewell'. Tonight, we come to the Lord with thanksgiving for the lives of two people – Tusi and his grandma, Mepa. Tonight, is a night of a happy farewell to Mepa, and also to Tusi." Wondering what the pastor meant, people whispered questions to each other so there was shush for quietness. "Firstly, we are here to celebrate and be happy to say farewell to Mepa because she has been called and is now on her journey to eternal life in heaven." There was silence and eagerness to hear the message from the pastor as he took a long pause to gather his emotions. "Secondly, we are here to celebrate and be happy to say farewell to Tusi because he has been called and is leaving on Sunday to study overseas." There were sounds of surprise because most people had assumed Tusi had come because of the death of his grandma. Others, especially the parents and relatives of Tusi, had thought that Tusi had just come to visit and was coincidently present at the time of the death of his grandma. To confirm what he had said, the pastor asked, "Is that right, that you are leaving on Sunday to study overseas Tusi?"

Everybody was quiet as a very emotional Tusi nodded his head in agreement and said, "With all my due respect, that is true pastor."

The pastor continued, "I am sure you all comforted Tusi by saying 'be brave' because he has just missed his Grandma who passed away at about 4.00 pm today. Now, given the great news about Tusi, we should all continue to comfort Tusi by saying 'be brave' because on his mission overseas he will not see his parents, family and friends for a long while and most importantly he will not see his grandma in this world ever again."

After the service, people who had caught up with the news came forward and placed their flowers in front of Grandma. Tusi sat by his grandma and opened the new suitcase he had bought for his parents. As everybody watched, Tusi took out the new clothes and the new hat and placed them on the dead body of his grandma. Weeping, he said, "Grandma, these are yours." With no answer from Grandma, Tusi questioned the dead body, "Come on Grandma, answer. Don't you like what I brought for you? I wouldn't have been able to get these things without your direction and help Grandma." Tusi placed the lace around the face of Grandma and the small wooden cross on her chest. He kissed his grandma's forehead, saying as he wept, "Thank you, so much for your love in directing me to have the *ake*, the liver to work hard. Now, I think that hard work as you wanted is paying off to some extent. At least we can now afford to buy *pisupo* to eat – instead of chicken shit as you always warned and challenged me when you got disappointed with me. I love you Grandma. Have a good trip."

Tusi had a few minutes after the formal service to brief his parents of the enormous blessings he suddenly received. To help his parents and family while away, Tusi bought a parcel of land within the Apia town area so his father could build a small house for them when going to town. Additionally, Tusi set up a special bank account where the rest of his pay would go to for his parents' general expenses. It appeared that the receiving of the scholarship was in time for Tusi to pay all the expenses for his Grandma, who contributed so much in his upbringing, funeral.

"The news of your going overseas is a shockingly surprise to us and all the people in our village. This is an amazing son - thanks to the Lord."

"Yes, Dad and Mum, only God knows, and I really don't understand and know how I got these blessings. I tried hard and did well in school and got a job all right as you know. You advised me last week about my marriage deal and I decided to stop but keep knocking to God through praying to show and explain to me His love while I am waiting for His direction. But now, see the amazing love of God!"

"Good to hear that you knocked to seek help from God through praying."

"Yes dad, and after a week of waiting for the Lord in His timing provide not just, but abundantly – not only cheap but completely free. I didn't have to chase any army like the Arameans to get the free study, land, house, and money, travelling and all – what a supernatural supply?"

Father emotionally responded, "Praise the Lord and give Him thanks and all the glory for the provision. Thank you, son, for whatever you set up for us before going – that is a great help. However, while we dearly appreciate the free provision from the Lord, we must keep praying to God for guidance so that we can wisely use the blessings. Last week son, I spoke to you about God's timing without knowing God's plan. I believe, this surprise call is a message from God that it is not time yet for you to have children. God knows that you need to climb a few mountains to equip yourself in caring and looking after a family in future - you need further education, experience more of His creation in other countries, meet new people and learn more on how to live a happy and experience sad situations in life."

"What a great free opportunity Dad. I am looking forward to going without fear for I know and believe the Lord is with us."

"Great to hear that son; while enjoying whatever overseas, show the Lord that you are using His blessing to serve Him through serving other people in those countries."

Emotionally, mother Kika advised, "This blessing makes me happy in front of the Lord. Keep praying to the Lord and He will help and look after you. I love you son."

"Thanks, Mum and Dad. I believe all these things we suddenly acquire are the reward of your love on us children. Pray God will look after you while I will be away, love you both."

How Tusi and parents receive these blessings was beyond their imagination and understanding. In their hearts, they thanked and praised the All-Mighty God.

Early Saturday morning, Tusi could not stay for the burial service of his grandma or he would miss the ferry to Apia. For the last time, Tusi kissed the lips and said goodbye to the dead body of Grandma. Likewise, he went around kissing and saying farewell to his parents, relatives, friends, and everyone else present. In saying goodbye his father advised, "Fear the Lord and love other people. Remember your prayer to God all the time. Be brave. I love you son, tofa."

"Thanks, Dad. I love you, tofa."

Emotionally, mother farewells her son saying; "Be brave son, the Lord is with you. I will miss you. I love you son -tofa."

"Thank you, mum. I will miss you too. Love you mum, tofa."

At about 8.30 am on Saturday morning it was time for Tusi to leave or else he would miss the last ferry from Loga to Fanua wharf in the afternoon. Therefore, he could not stay for the burial service of his grandma. For the last time, Tusi kissed the lips and said goodbye to the dead body of Grandma. Likewise, he went around kissing and saying farewell to his parents, relatives, friends and everyone else present. All encouraged Tusi to be brave in his mission.

Acknowledgement

I am indebted to my grandma and my parents, sisters, brothers, relatives and friends for the great help and support during my life, on which this novel is based.

With many thanks to:

My family at Avao - Lotoaso and Avea, Afereti, Saifoloi, Leitu, Toe and Faáfao. Paletaoga and Amata, Otineru, Suésuévale, Aso, Epati and others;

My friends at Vaipouli College and SPRCTA: Fuifui Taotua, Ken Lameta, Sauiluma Kupa, Liva Chriton, Eteri Fereti, Ionatana L Fasavalu, Taálo Lauofo, Malo Tokoma, Tavita Moala, Ioane Fa'asavalu, Ioane Aloali'i, Mataerangi Purea, Bob and others;

My editor Roxana Coumans from Germany; My Book Cover Designer : top_hit_design from Pakistan; and

My formatting agent: Zahidulsajib from Bangladesh.

God bless you all.

Pasene Tauialo: saveapt@gmail.com

www.ingramcontent.com/pod-product-compliance
Lightning Source LLC
Chambersburg PA
CBHW072126270326
41931CB00010B/1681